That men do not learn very much from the lessons of history
is the most important of all the lessons of history.
— Aldous Huxley

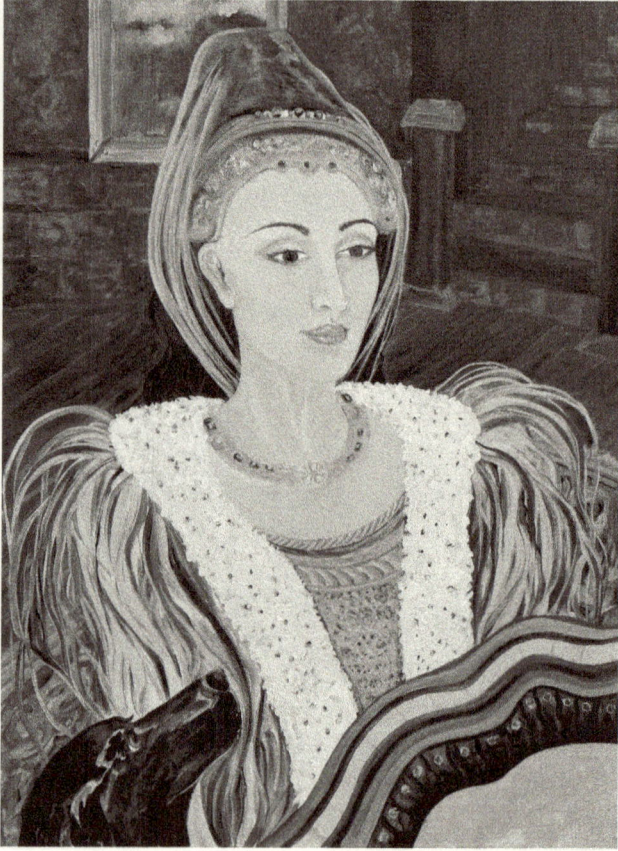

Lady Eleanor Talbot

A Dream
Within A Dream

Clarence W. Padgett

Lantern Publications
Hagensborg, BC, Canada

A Dream Within A Dream

A Lantern Publications / Turning Point Arts Book

All rights reserved.
Copyright © 2008-2017 by Clarence W. Padgett.

The cover portrait of Lady Eleanor Talbot was painted
by Theresa Thomas, Hagensborg, BC.

The photograph of the cover portrait for printing was
taken by Michael Wigle, Hagensborg, BC.

Book design and pre-press by Brad Grigor, Turning Point Arts.
www.turningpointarts.com

Library and Archives Canada Cataloguing in Publication
Padgett, Wayne, 1941-, author
    A dream within a dream / Clarence W. Padgett.

Includes bibliographical references and index.
ISBN 978-0-9939287-1-0 (softcover)

    1. Talbot, Eleanor, 1436-1468. 2. Edward IV, King of
England, 1442-1483. 3. Spouses of heads of state--Great
Britain--Biography. 4. Queens--Great Britain--Biography.
5. Edward IV, King of England, 1442-1483--Relations with
women. 6. Great Britain--History--Edward IV, 1461-1483.

    I. Title.

DA258.P33 2017   942.044092   C2017-900937-0

Printed in Canada

Special thanks go to my wife, Sie, for assisting me with her support in the writing of this book. I dedicate this book to her with much love and respect.

Contents

Contents *(continued)*

Preface

What I have attempted to accomplish in this publication is best explained in the following quote:

"In the words and deeds of the past, there lies hidden a treasure that people may use to strengthen and elevate their characters. The way to study the past is not to confine oneself to the mere knowledge of history but, through the application of this knowledge, to give actuality to the past."*

*The I Ching or Book of Changes, No. 26, Bollingen Series XIX, ©1950 by Bollingen Foundation Inc., New York, NY. Published by Princeton University Press, Princeton, NJ.

A Dream
Within A Dream

CHAPTER ONE
The New Beginning

This book was developed around a group of four dreams. I am the "dreamer" and main storyteller. One of my favorite writers is Edgar Allan Poe, who had lived in the city of Richmond, Virginia in the early 1800s. In fact, Poe's home can still be seen there today. Because of the nature of my dreams, I have taken the title for this manuscript from a collection of Poe's work. It is from a poem entitled *A Dream Within A Dream*, and the first part of the poem goes like this:[1]

> *Take this kiss upon the brow!*
> *And, in parting from you now,*
> *This much let me avow—*
> *You are not wrong, who deem*
> *That my days have been a dream;*
> *Yet if hope has flown away*
> *In a night or in a day,*
> *In a vision, or in none,*
> *Is it therefore the less gone?*
> *All that we see or seem*
> *Is but a dream within a dream.*

The story of these dreams left me with a feeling that this was a once-in-a-lifetime occasion. However, it took me a long time before I could gain enough courage or mental clarity to even try to begin putting this story together. I discussed the first dream with my wife and asked her what she thought I should do with what I had experienced. She didn't discourage me in any way, but she said that I had to make my own decision. I was afraid to tell my closest friends about these dreams for fear they might think I had really gone over the top this time. In fact, I wasn't quite sure of that myself.

I can't remember now how long it took me after the first dream occurred to start even trying to put this story together from the notes I had collected. I didn't know if the first dream was just a fluke and an isolated incident or not. I didn't think I had enough information on which to build a story, so I just put everything aside and went on with my life.

I had documented this first dream as occurring in early November 1994. From my initial studies of some of the historical information I had from the main body of the dream, I discovered that it took place at Sudeley Castle, near Winchcomb, Gloucestershire, England.[2] The main character in this dream was a woman named Eleanor who explained that she was the mother of young Edward de Wigmore.

I experienced the second dream in late December of 1994, about two months after the first dream. When it occurred, I thought it was too strange to be true. I barely had time to recover from the shock and wonder why this was all happening when a third dream came in February of 1995. The fourth and final dream occurred in early April of 1995.

I view this final dream as the homecoming dream. It covered young Edward's connection with a woman named Jane de Wigmore, of de Wigmore Castle, and the FitzOsberne clan in Wales, in the 1460s.[3] It contained segments of the other dreams to round out the whole story. It was so interwoven with the other three dreams in this group that I finally had to write it in three parts to make the whole story easier to follow. Creating this order was a difficult and frustrating task. The dreams did not occur in an orderly fashion. Much of the story came to me in fragments. None of these dreams came to me as just ordinary dreams. They all seemed to demand my undivided attention. During the four dreams that make up this whole story, I don't remember ever being interrupted by any ancillary or ordinary dreams. I was grateful for that. I had a hard enough time to just sort out what I had experienced already.

After the first dream, I realized I was half awake and mentally and physically drained. I managed to turn on the light and look at the clock; it was 3:00 a.m. I did go back to sleep because I was so exhausted. I woke again at about 8:00 a.m. that same morning and began to jot down some highlights of that initial dream. At first I started recording it from raw memory with pen and paper with a lot of notes scribbled in the margins. I outlined any tiny bit of information I could remember. I felt helpless because I didn't know where to start. In fact, I wasn't sure I even wanted to start. There was seemingly so much information and I already felt I had lost most of it. I had lots of doubt as to whether this was just a fluke and a one-time experience.

I remember feeling overwhelmed when I first became aware that this dream was starting to happen. I became worried when I experienced an involuntary interaction with the dream. I felt I was being dragged by my feet into some very unfamiliar territory. I remember saying to myself in the beginning, "Why is all this coming to me? I'm not the least bit interested in all this history; I just want to go back to sleep!" Then, some compelling energy let me know I should pay close attention to what was unfolding. The rest is history, literally, which you will read about in this writing.

I want you, the reader, to know that I did, at certain points, give up on this project. I just wanted to put this all behind me and forget it ever happened. After I calmed down some, I started thinking these dreams were so unusual that there must be some reason this message was coming to me in such a vivid expression.

The story seemed so convoluted, with layer upon layer of history that I honestly cared nothing about, as I have already alluded to. Also, there were many things happening in my personal life at that time. Reality called and I realized I had to try to go on with what is referred to as "making a living." I knew I didn't have time to get involved in some off-the-wall dream. Then, as you will see, I did decide to start finding out about my own ancestral background. I was curious to see if there might be any bits of information pertaining to these dreams I had just had to lend some guidance to my situation.

The first dream, as I see it, now that I have put these four dreams and some of the research together, was a focal point for this whole story. I tried, out of habit, to place everything in a neat, linear order, but that wasn't the way the story really came together, right from the beginning.

I worked on this for many weeks. As the story began to pour out, I realized there seemed to be some sort of underlying natural order to what I was finding. The more I began to find out about my past, the more it led to other findings. I began finding names that were showing up in my research of the dreams. It was so odd that these dreams, as strange as it seemed, would come to me. I believe that because this was such an out-of-the-ordinary situation, my imagination teased me into taking part in it.

When I had gone as far as I could go with the basic story, it still wasn't in what I would call an understandable format. It felt as though I was writing a thesis. I tried to place the dreams in a neat, linear order: dream number one, then add dream two, then dream three and, finally, dream four. As I was trying to edit my rough notes, I realized that this was not how the story had been presented to me from the beginning.

The story started taking shape after I knew the first dream was not just an isolated event. I began to see it as the center of the whole story. It presented fragments of information that contained some of the main issues of the other dreams. Later on, I had to find a method to write this manuscript to make a flowing transition to connect all four of these dreams. I finally realized the story I was trying to tell had to be written in the first person, with me telling the story. Because I had never witnessed anything like this, my biggest problem of all was where to begin. I realized if I wanted to try to write a readable story, I had a big task ahead of me—the dreams were so complicated, I knew I didn't understand them myself yet. I knew I had to put it all together in a readable format to create a story the reader could follow.

I was driven to find out more about Jane de Wigmore, mentioned by Eleanor as being her son's adoptive mother. So, then I realized that this was how the other dreams came about as well. I had to focus on the first dream all through this whole process. I needed to get answers as to who all the other characters were, besides Eleanor, Jane and young Edward, and how they were a part of a life I was unknowingly revisiting.

The second dream, as I have mentioned, occurred almost two months after the first dream. It had occurred just before Christmas in 1994 and I was totally shocked! "How could this be happening to me again?" I thought. The shock consisted also of feelings of "Oh no, here we go again," and "Am I losing my mind?" Then, "I'm right back were I was in that other dream!" I suddenly felt the urge to get out of all this. I had felt that in the first dream. These dreams seemed to be invading my whole life. I felt as though I had no control of this situation. I was being dragged into this dream the same way I started in the first dream. When I realized I had no control in these dreams, I also realized that is how I try to organize my own life. I feel that if I'm not in control of what I'm doing, I can't function. That is why I think I like to be self-employed and always be my own boss.

So now it seemed that I had at some point unintentionally encouraged this second dream to happen, without realizing it. I would go to sleep thinking about who Jane de Wigmore was. I wanted to know what part she represented in the dreams. At this point, I also wanted to know what she had to do with my personal history, if anything. I had never come in contact with her name anywhere, not even in the family history I was starting to collect. I knew for sure that these dreams were not just ordinary dreams. For the first time, I felt relatively sure there was a story starting to take place here. I still wasn't convinced I wanted to get involved with all of this. The next thing I had to do was try to find out why this dream had come back again in almost the same identical format as the first dream. I didn't feel I was any further ahead in understanding any of this. In the beginning of this second dream, I thought I was being victimized. I was uncomfortable but at the same time I was captivated by the mysteriousness of it all. The second dream didn't repeat the first dream. It began where the first dream had ended. Just as in our daily life, the story picked up where it had left off.

I still had so many questions left over from the first dream. I felt I needed some answers from that dream before I could pay close attention to what was happening next. I felt I was beginning to receive so much information, I didn't know what to do with it all.

To my amazement, as this second dream progressed, it seemed it was no longer so traumatic this time. Lady Eleanor had explained in a fragment from the first dream how young Edward, her son, came to be adopted by Jane de Wigmore. This fact caused me to want to know more about his adoptive mother. Surprisingly, this part of the dreams turned out to be a mellow and wonderful experience. As Jane portrayed her role in the second dream, I was able to transfer that information to some more of the writing. This dream left me with a feeling that this was an event of my lifetime.

Now I knew this wasn't just some "incidental nightmare." I had come out of this second dream realizing that this had become another awakening event with its own unique merits. I couldn't wait to see where this was going to take me next. I had found the transition I needed to answer my lingering questions. I began to believe this was perhaps becoming a view of a previous life experience I may have once had with these same people I was dreaming about. Then the transition I took from this second dream seemed to lead me very naturally to experience the next segment of this story.

The third dream seemed to evolve from the first and second dreams. I realized I was with characters who were becoming familiar. I couldn't recall ever having dreams about the same characters over again. I seemed to know what to expect when I realized this new dream was happening. It was becoming apparent to me that one dream seemed to be setting up the next dream to happen. I didn't have to make up anything; it was all there for me to watch it happen. These weren't just dreams of scattered, random events; these images I was receiving were like movie sets. They were organized and the characters in those sets knew their lines and spoke them clearly and with certainty. It was about this same time that I began to realize some of the fragments in these dreams could be interpreted as a type of code to let me know what I needed to research next. I was able to use that idea to a great advantage. When I had the first dream and I made an attempt to start gathering the historical material I thought I would need to start with, I was all over the place. I started out with a pile of material I had to sift through and I still didn't know where I should start. Then I learned, from these "fragment codes," what questions to try to answer and in what order they belonged. I now had more of an idea of the order that information should be placed in to give the story its own rhythm.

I came to a place in the dreams where Lady Eleanor's son, young Edward de Wigmore, was about seven years old. He was being sent by his adoptive mother, Jane de Wigmore, to live with a man who would take him to meet his birth mother. Because he had been adopted as an infant, he had no memory of her.

Lorne was a farmer who supplied Sudeley Castle and other castles around his area with produce from his gardens. Jane and Lorne had friends in common and had known each other for some years. Jane had gotten word to Lorne to ask him to take young Edward to see Lady Eleanor, during one of his deliveries to Sudeley Castle.

Young Edward had no idea he was going there to see his mother. He had been told he was going to stay with a friend of Jane's, because there was so much fighting going on in Wales at that time. Edward knew this was true because he had grown up in that way of life. This would be a total surprise for him. This would be the only time he would see his mother, since Jane had taken him and raised him for about seven years.

So this was part of my third dream, but now I began to realize the dreams had taken me full circle back into the first dream as well! The dreams all seemed interwoven through each other. That is why I decided to entitle this manuscript *A Dream Within A Dream*, because that was definitely what I saw developing. These dreams each seemed to be brief fleeting moments in "real time." The main characteristic of each of these dreams so far was that each dream seemed independently unique. Each time I had a new dream I would always use the previous dream as a reference point. Then when the dreams ended, all the dreams were interconnected as one whole story. I knew I wasn't finished and all I had was a basic outline of where the story was proceeding. I still didn't know if there would be any more dreams. I didn't have time to think about there being more dreams—I had to spend my time working on what I already had.

In the first dream, I saw young Edward de Wigmore as he was standing in a vivid brightness of an early morning sun with shadows still lingering. He could see a shadow of himself standing in the main hall of an ancient castle. This scene reminded him of his growing up at such a place similar to that at his home castle on Mount Snowdon.

I began to do some research on Sudeley Castle. I found there really was such a place and it is still functioning. It is located near England's southeastern border with Wales, near the English town of Herefordshire and had been built in the 11th century. I didn't know anything about it but now I am fully aware of it and its long and mysterious history.[4]

When I realized my dreams had shown me something I could call "reality," I was totally shocked and amazed! For the first time I knew my dreams had an actual basis, founded in the recorded history of England and Wales. This brought me some mixed emotions. I was excited and bewildered at the same time.

At first, I didn't know which way to turn. I felt my mind was playing tricks on me and I became afraid. I began to doubt myself again. I knew the dreams had shown me something real, something supposedly tangible, that I could at least refer to and see in printed pictures and words. Slowly, I started regaining my confidence. That, I believe, became the main impetus for me to want to go on and pursue this undertaking.

Now I seemed to have enough footing in what we call reality to allow me to go ahead and see what I could make of this experience. I wondered if my always avoiding this historic period had caused me to become attached to it. I finally became fascinated by this phenomenon of being able to have dreams of certain historical events, even if it was from the Middle Ages, and then find these events in the actual written history.

As a twelve-year-old child, I had already had a similar kind of experience, as will be mentioned in chapter two. These dreams I was experiencing now were far more detailed than in my "one-on-one" experience as a child. These dreams were longer and they were in far more intricate detail.

In this series of dreams, at first, I felt as though I was watching myself and the activities of the day happening around me. Even so, I was aware that my ego would only let me see myself, at first, as just a one person audience. In the first dream I was not taking, or wanting to take, an active part in any of the activities or be involved with the people I first encountered there. I began to enjoy just being a bystander, watching what was taking place.

From my perspective, there seemed to be an ongoing contradiction in the story that was being told. I would realize later on where this feeling was coming from. When I first started having these dreams, they seemed so fragmented, but as they progressed I became more familiar with the story that was being acted out. I began to see a natural pattern in the events that were unfolding. I remember feeling as though I was being compelled by some hidden force to take some role in what I thought I was observing taking place. Somehow, I realized I should pay close attention to what was happening. I was beginning to see these dreams, as a sort of "subconscious awareness."

When I look back on this time as a whole, I remember these four dreams as having the most clear images and sounds of any dreams I have ever experienced! During the first dream, the images I began experiencing seemed as though I was looking through a hole in reality, which I had discovered when the first dream began to materialize. Then, I began to want to keep watching to see what would happen next and to not miss any part of what seemed to be unfolding.

From taking a closer look through that so called "hole," I suddenly realized I was dreaming. I was shocked to realize this. I felt there was some reason why I was being singled out to watch what was beginning to happen. I began to feel panicked, hot and restless, when I realized I was dreaming, but I knew also I was attracted to the images I was see-ing. I then became conscious of being able to logically reason and take what I viewed as only a part-time role in what became this first dream.

Then, the tempo of the dream changed when young Edward heard a woman crying upstairs at a giant castle he was in. He felt a sudden urge to help her, because she sounded so sad. It seemed that he had to become involved in what was taking place there, whether he wanted to or not. He seemed to be drawn and committed to reach out to the woman in some way.

That is why, as the dreams kept occurring, I still functioned with what I call a "fear edge." I felt as though I was filming a movie. I felt present but invisible. I could see the characters but they could not see me. At first, for awhile, this edge still gave me a way to either take part in or not take part in what I was sensing was happening. At the time I was going through this first dream, I didn't realize when this dream ended, that others would follow. I could barely compre-hend what seemed later to be only a small part of this whole series of dreams.

At first, I thought I could have stopped the dreams when they started getting too uncomfortable for me but now I'm not sure of that. I don't know if I could have stopped these dreams from continuing or not. I don't know why, at times, I wanted to stop the dreams. I think it was because I couldn't figure out what they had to do with me. Maybe it was my self-centeredness that caused me to feel that way. This was a crucial point for my involvement in these dreams.

I remember wanting to end these dreams, because I had come out of the first dream feeling so uncomfortable with a lingering thought of *How could my mind let this happen to me?* At times I felt a nagging feeling of being mentally victimized by some of the dreaming. I felt I was sent there as a witness to this whole event. I couldn't figure out why I was there. I felt I had no part to play except to serve as an observer.

I don't know even now, if we choose our dreams or perhaps, our dreams choose us. To answer my own question, I don't know if there is a definite answer to that question. When I was having the first dream, I tried to maintain the perogative to cancel it if I thought it was getting too heavy, mentally or physically, to handle any more. That emotion didn't last long. Soon after that first dream began, I seemed to be swept along with the activities that were taking place. I didn't know if it was being directed at me, or if it was just a mixture of the activities of my day. It appeared the dream was its own entity with a mission to fulfill. It seemed to be determined to happen, whether I was willing to acknowledge it or not. So, I finally decided to go with it and see where it would lead me. The presence of its form, color, sound, and movement was something that caught and held my attention. I have never experienced that feeling in my dreams before or since.

When I first realized my attention was focused on the images I was seeing, suddenly I wasn't able to linger on any certain image for very long. Everything seemed to be moving quickly. Later, as the first dream progressed, I couldn't understand why sometimes the dream seemed to move so quickly and at other times it seemed to be almost standing still. Then I felt I was getting ready to play a part in all this. I don't know what convinced me to even try that, let alone what role I should, or would, play if any. I recognized that feeling from being in all my grade school plays. I didn't know if I would even have a choice here. From then on, mostly in the second dream, every movement at first seemed to be in "slow motion" but even then I could hardly take it all in. When I learned to relax in whatever dream I was experiencing, I felt as though I was in a suspended state of wonderment. At times my fear of these dreams seemed to subside.

Then, if I felt I was relaxing too much, after I started viewing the images so clearly, I would start feeling I was getting into something I couldn't understand. When that feeling began to overcome me, I had a sudden urge to "run away" and just forget what I was seeing but the dream now had my attention. I couldn't let it go. I was captivated by what I was experiencing, good or bad. I began to feel there was some sort of message here from which to learn. I knew, even in this dream state, that this event was something new that I might never have a chance to experience again. In fact, I have not had even a flash of any of those four basic dreams revisit me since they stopped happening in April of 1995. I have not had any dreams to compare with those before or since then.

I realized in these dreams how prevalent the feeling of running away, when things got too tough, has been with me for most of my life. This feeling of wanting to leave when things in my everyday life become too complicated, is still very much with me today.

So, this experience is the outcome of my having become open to what I was being shown. I realize now I am no longer afraid of my dreams. I have in fact learned to rely on my "historical intuition" and will be working on a sequel to this work, using some of the methods I have developed here to help me discover more about the history from my past. I hope you enjoy reading this as much as I have writing it. I am excited to see where it may lead me next.

I want to share this with the readers of this work. At times, when I have been deeply involved in the research necessary to put this whole project together, I would question myself. I would mainly question how and why I had become a part of this whole story.

The only answer I could ascertain was that there was information hidden deep within my psyche from a life that I had lived long ago. I have now realized I was being bathed in a history that had taken place all around me in a time past. Now since I have experienced these historical dreams, there seems to be no end to the information I am discovering from the written history for this manuscript and perhaps others in the future. I have found our dreams can be a wealth of knowledge for us.

CHAPTER TWO
The Life Of The Child Dreamer

I remember my youth fondly. Family enjoyed my dancing a jig as they played their music. I could make my grandpa laugh until he had tears in his eyes. That was certainly a special time in my life. I felt as though the world was there for my enjoyment. When I was six years old, my family moved out to the country. The first thing I wanted was a dog and I got one. My dad got me a little Toy Manchester and I named her, Teency, because she was so very small. She would go with me anywhere I wanted to go. She was my faithful companion until she got run over by a car, chasing after me. I buried her in a small black suitcase in center field of my ball diamond, where all of us kids used to play ball.

Across the road from my home there was a big field and an old farmhouse where some people still lived that were looking after the place. My dad asked them if he could grow a field of corn there and they said yes. My dad went out and got an old gray mule to plow the field, just as he had done when he was a young boy. The neighbor kids and I used to ride that mule. My dad saw we were having so much fun he let me go ahead. We had a fine time even when we got going so fast we fell off. My dad found an old walking plow he could use with the mule. He plowed part of that big field with that mule just like he had done with his father when he was young. He planted his corn there.

I remember the time I was walking out through the cornfield after a rain. I was looking down at the ground as I walked and suddenly spotted my first arrowhead. That opened a whole new world for me. I had never found or even seen anything like that before. I was so excited, I couldn't believe what I was seeing and I was surrounded by these in the environment I grew up in.[1]

I found out later that the small white stone was called quartz. It was perfectly notched at the bottom, making it possible to fasten it to a stick with animal hide strings. I knelt down and picked it up. Then, I held it in my hands and studied it. I don't know how long I held it in my gaze. I still have a vague memory of where in that field I found it. I treasured it as though it was some sort of jewel.

As I gazed at it and admired its perfection, I thought to look around to see if anyone was watching me. At first, it was as though I didn't want anyone to know I had found such a beautiful piece of carved stone I didn't know was so ancient. I realized it had been made by a person long ago. I didn't want anyone to know where I had found it. It became my secret. I became very possessive of it, like my secret treasure.

From finding that one arrowhead, I felt a new kind of self-worth. I knew I was going to learn about something I didn't know was there. I was going to make that my new school. I thought, *I may not be able to read like all the other kids, but none of them have found an arrowhead.* When I finally showed it to my classmates, they just looked at it and I read in their expression, *So what, it's just a piece of white stone made into a shape.* No one seemed to be the least bit interested in it. From then on, I always went arrowhead hunting on my own.

All I could think about it was that it was a primitive person fashioning that stone with their own hands. I had never seen anything like it. I thought in my child's mind that these things were only found in museums, not just lying out there scattered out on the ground for me to discover.

I reckoned someone with the proper skills had turned this piece of stone into a tool they could use for hunting or to defend themselves. I wondered, how old could this arrowhead be. When I got into the higher grades, I started asking around at school and one teacher told me it was from The Stone Age. I asked him, "How far back would that be?" and he said, "Oh, probably about ten thousand years ago would be when they would have made tools out of stone." I told him I couldn't think that far back. As time went on, I would find a whole collection of arrowheads. I used to sleep with them under my pillow hoping to have dreams of the people who had made them, so I could see how they lived and did things then.

I remember one day when I felt I needed to take time to myself and be quiet. Teency and I went to look for arrowheads. I never asked other kids to go out with me anymore because none of them seemed interested in looking for arrowheads. I used that time as my kind of meditation. Even if I didn't happen to find any arrowheads when I went out, just the anticipation of maybe finding even one still made it an exciting activity for me and my dog. That simple pursuit cost me nothing. I realized as I got older, I had used my arrowhead hunting as kind of my own personal therapy when things were going downhill with my parents' relationship with each other.

Later on as I got better at finding the arrowheads, I also started finding small ceramic balls that looked like marbles. I didn't find many of them but I took the ones I had found around to some of the old timers in my area. I asked them if they could tell me what these little round balls were. The first old farmer I approached said, "Those are called 'mini-shot,' son." Then he went on to say, "When the Confederate Army in the southern US was running out of ammunition in fighting the Union Armies of the northern US, they had to start making their own bullets out of high-fired clay. They did that so they wouldn't crack when the hammer hit them and shot them from their rifles." Then he said, as he pointed it out, "See the little mark on the ball there? That shows it was fired from a rifle and that is the mark from the hammer hitting the shot to fire it." I couldn't believe what he had just taught me. I made sure to thank him for showing me that. There was another piece of recent history, right at my doorstep. All of those experiences of finding artifacts all around me as a very young child makes me happy to recall them, even now. When I was still a child, my father once told me, "You are a dreamer." I didn't know at that time what he meant, but I think I do now.

CHAPTER THREE
My Personal Vision As A Child

As I had mentioned earlier as a child first starting out in school, I couldn't read. I used to cry because I ended up in the lowest reading group. Finally, my mother sat down with me and taught me how to read but that wasn't until fourth grade in a little country school. I was raised in the Southern Baptist Church and I would often practice my reading skills by reading scriptures from the Bible. I found, in my studies of the Bible, the *Book of Revelations* to be the most interesting to me. When I used to ask our preachers how those "revelations" had come about they would all tell me, "These were all divinely inspired messages from God."

From that information I used to wonder what these people that wrote down prophesies were like, and what kind of life they had lived. I also wanted to know how they were accepted by their society. I always had a feeling that preachers I would question thought I was too young to even ask those kind of questions, so I learned early on to keep those kind of questions to myself. I know this may be considered a little out of the ordinary for a child of ten years old, but even then I was thinking of becoming a Baptist minister someday, so I wanted to learn as much as I could about the people who wrote the Bible.

When I was twelve years old I had a strange experience. I suppose it could be referred to as a revelation or quickening or divine inspiration or a vision. The scene for this mental experience was a hot summer afternoon and I had just finished mowing the lawn with our old push mower. I had gone in the house to have some iced tea. To relax, I had gone into my bedroom and sat down at a table I had set up in there. This is where I kept my school books and did my homework.

As I sat there, I reached for my Bible and began to thumb through the pages. Suddenly I was frightened by what seemed to be an overwhelming message. I thought right away the message I was receiving was only audible to me. Still, I had no idea where this message was coming from or how to respond to it. I quickly assumed it must be a message from heaven or some spiritual place. Because I was there by myself I just assumed I would be the one to take the message. My mother and sister had gone to town that morning.

I had never experienced anything like that before. All I was really sure of at that moment was I knew I wasn't dreaming and I became captivated by the message that was coming to me. I didn't think I had a choice not to listen. The sound was louder than a phone call and the tone was demanding. There seemed to be an inference, as I understood it, that this message, whatever it was, would only be given once.

When the message came, I couldn't find any paper or anything to write with on my table, which was not usual for me. This had caught me completely off guard, with no warning at all. I never expected anything like this to happen in my life. I vaguely remember laying my Bible down on the table. For some reason, I placed my hands on my face and covered my eyes. I had a mental impulse to shut out everything present, so I could totally concentrate on what was very rapidly being told to me. I wanted to clear my mind of everything but that message.

Somehow, I was able to pull myself together enough to begin listening to this message which went as follows: "You will know that some drastic changes are going to take place upon the earth when you see these major events happening. There will be an invention that sends messages in letter form directly from the source to anyone's office or home." I tried to think how that could possibly be done in 1953, but later on I knew that was the fax machine and now we have e-mail.

I was barely able to register that thought in my twelve-year-old mind when another message was on the way. The next message said, "Another invention to watch for is a machine that a person appearing on a screen can be seen and talked with by the person talking to them."

I couldn't even begin to consider that statement then but now I know that was television. Now it is Blackberry, etc.

Then the tone of the message suddenly changed to a political genre that said, "You will know that great changes are about to happen in the world when the political ideologies between Communism and Democracy become as one." Now, I didn't know what Communism was until my father used to call some of the American presidents Communists, when I was about ten years old. I had some idea that Democracy was the way of life in the US and Canada.

Then, suddenly the message ended. I don't know how long it was after the message ended, before I got up from my table and started moving around. I didn't know how long that message lasted. I felt completely drained. I suddenly realized I was still in the house alone. Again, I was glad I was alone because it gave me time to settle down and try to recover from what I had just experienced. After having time to come back to my normal self, I wondered how many young people, or people of all ages, ever had this sort of occurrence happen to them and would they ever tell anyone about it.

My mother and sister came home from town that late afternoon. I didn't want my sister to know what I had just experienced because she was very young and I thought it would have been difficult to explain it to her, and I thought at the time it might just frighten her. When I was able to get my mother alone, I tried to explain to her what I had experienced. She could see that I was still shaken by what had happened when I was trying to relate this story to her.

After I had explained my experience to her, she seemed surprised but not shocked. She was not an excitable person. She would take in what was being said and think about it, before she would comment. Then, in her kind way and soft voice, she said, "Things like this happen to some people at times." I thanked her for talking to me and gave her a hug and asked her not to tell my dad, because he might think it was too weird. She told me she would keep it to herself. She did, and I never talked about again, to anyone.

For a long time after that experience, I had wondered what I would have done if anyone had come into the house at the time this message was unfolding. I was alone there and I was glad. I thought, *How would I have ever explained something like that to anyone other than my mother?* Later on, I wondered if I would have even had that message come to me if anyone else was there to hear it? I was plenty frightened as it was. I felt as though I was caught between the feelings of being too young to be going through something like this and being totally mystified by that experience. This message came to me in 1953 when I was twelve years old. Somehow, and I didn't understand how, the message I received was in English. I wondered about that for quite some time afterwards. I wondered if messages like that happened in other countries, would it be given in the language of that country? I was afraid to ask anybody that question and so I just let it go. Eventually, I forgot that whole episode, that is until I had these dreams I'm writing about here.

CHAPTER FOUR
Collecting A View Of My Ancestors

S hortly after I had experienced my first dream which makes up a large portion of this story, in November of 1994, I had word there was going to be a book show at a mall near where I was living at that time. I decided to go and see if I could find some books to do some research about the Middle Ages. I never thought I would be buying books on that subject. I was able to find some new books and some from a used bookstore where I had found books I needed before. I'll discuss some of the books I found to help me with this project later on.

When I was getting ready to leave the mall, I noticed a table where several people were sitting. As I passed by their table I glanced at what they were selling. I couldn't believe it; they were printing up and selling documents showing family Coats of Arms, with a brief summary of the history of the various family names. So, I decided to get the documents for both Paget, my grandfather's family, and Boddie, or Bothie in Welsh, for my grandmother's family history in Wales. I couldn't wait to get home and read them to see just what my ancestral background might look like. I suddenly took a greater interest in my family history since I had now had these dreams. Neither my father nor my mother ever mentioned much about their family histories. When I started working on this manuscript, I didn't know if my parents ever knew how to find this kind of information or if they just weren't interested in what may have happened in their past.[1]

I found out about land my father's family was granted, from some family papers my sister had come across a few years ago. My father always used to say he was not related to any of that royalty in England. As I have now found out, we are very much related to the royalty of England, Ireland and Wales and have ancient roots with them all.

For some reason I was always interested in where my ancestors came from but when you are young, you don't know how to go about finding any of that information and generally lose interest after awhile. When I finally arrived home I proudly showed off the documents and the few books I had found. My wife is not big on history but she was happy that I had found some books and information that might help me with my research. So I went to read some of the new material I had bought.

I began to read my Coat of Arms and found that the name Padgett (Paget) originated in Normandy, a district of France. It explained that our family name had originated in the town of Pachet in Normandy. I looked for that town on modern maps but could not find it. Certain members of my grandparents' families, I recently found out, had been with William the Conqueror at the Battle of Hastings, in 1066. That shows that these two families had known each other for over 900 years. They not only knew each other they had done business together for about half that long.

The Pagets settled first in Oxford county and later helped develop Oxford University. They became well educated parliamentarians and they stayed close to the various governments of England. They married into each others family in the early 1400s. They were rewarded for their services to the various kings and they prospered well for it.[2]

From that Coat of Arms document, I was able to contact a member of my ancestral family in England. My contact kindly sent me a letter and a booklet, showing the basic historical background of both of my grandfather's and my grandmother's families. The booklet I received offered some very interesting information. It contained my family's history back to the early 1300s. It also had a picture of a family castle located in Anglesey Isle, in northern Wales. The name of the castle was, and still is, Plas Newydd. I found that there had been several castles by that name in Wales. My family tree shows some of the owner/occupants to have been, Gwilym ap Gruffydd, Lord of Penrhyn, born 1365, died 1431. He supposedly died at age 66 in Austria-Hungary. This was one of my grandmother's direct ancestors. In my recent research I have found this man to be one of the last remaining descendants of Llewelyn ab Iorwerth, one of the last native Kings of Wales.

In further research, I found Gwilym's father, Gruffydd ap Gwilym, Lord of Penrhyn, born 1322 and died 1405 at age 83, in Austria-Hungary as well. I haven't found out where they are buried yet but I'm still researching that. I am still trying to find out why both of them would have given up their families and all their properties and just left and gone to Austria-Hungary, each in their own time. I found that they were both descendants of the old Tudor Kings, the same line as Henry VI. I haven't found out if they lived out their lives in Austria-Hungary or went on to some other place.[3] This is a project I've had to put on hold for now but I will work on it later. I have some theories, but no hard proof yet. This is just a small part of my own history I have come upon by doing research for the manuscript I'm working on now. That information will be pursued, hopefully in my next book.

When I wrote to a family member in England for information about our family, he explained that my name was spelled Padgett, unlike his, which he spelled Paget. I also realized that certain members of families were sometimes sent to fight in foreign fields as a type of discipline. I learned from the booklet I was sent that the line I am related to is Thomas 3rd Baron Paget, born 1544 died 1589. His son, also named Thomas, became a Catholic and was exiled to Ireland, but subsequently was sent to the Virginia Colony in 1639. I then found his name in my Coat of Arms spelled Padgett. I asked a relative in England why my name was not spelled Paget. He told me my name used the Tudor spelling meaning the family was "disfranchised" or, more plainly, cut out of the wealth of the family.

In doing my research for this manuscript I found out where that particular "ancestral break" took place. It was when William Paget was a privy councilor to Henry VIII who installed him in the Order of the Garter.

It was rumored that Henry wanted Paget to be the next king. This did not sit well with Elizabeth I when she became Queen. Paget then retired from political life.

The change in the spelling of names can be a demarcation sign and means a family line has been disfranchised. Usually the reasons would be of a political nature.

William Boddie, from my grandmother's family, helped sail the colonists to the eastern seaboard with ships in the family group known as *The White Sail Ships*. This was only part of the settlement plan; there still had to be the labor in place to clear the land and tend the crops in the wilderness of these new colonies. A labor force had to be put in place quickly.[4]

Recently I researched where the black slaves had come from that had been brought to Virginia. I found that most of them had been brought there from the west coast of Africa. They were mostly from the country of Ivory Coast or Cote D'ivoire. Historians at the University of Richmond explained that they could trace where they had come from because of the dialects they spoke.[5]

I discovered that my family who settled in Virginia named the county they lived in after the place they were from in England. My ancestors named their county, Isle of Wight.

The course of events would be: *The White Sail Ships* would leave Portsmouth, their home port in England, with a load of what was known then as "Prisoners of Old Mother England." These people would be freed when the ships got down into the west coast of Australia, so they could help start setting up a colony down there. The ships would then turn around and head back to the west coast of Africa. They were empty of cargo and would stop in at a port named Abidjan, which had a well protected inlet and harbor. That is where they would buy and load slaves that would be taken back to the Virginia colony and maybe some of the other colonies as well.[6]

In 1999, I was down in Australia, on the west coast near Perth. I had gone with a friend who was going to show me around. It was late September and getting very warm. We were in a store in a small town where we were staying for a few days and we were buying a few things. Suddenly one of the women clerks turned to me and said in a loud voice, "You called me a *pome!*" I was shocked and embarrassed. I had no idea of what she was accusing me. I told her right away that I hadn't call her that and I didn't even know what the word meant. My friend quickly escorted me outside, where he explained that "pome" was a derogatory term meaning "Prisoners of Old Mother England."

I have been asked many times in my life if I was Australian and I had always told them no. I didn't have anybody in my immediate families who had been Australian or had even been there, that I knew of. I always thought that was kind of strange. When I was in Australia I picked up the accent readily. I couldn't drive a vehicle there with the steering wheel on the right side and drive in the left lane. I was afraid I would use an "off-ramp" as an "on ramp." Everything about driving there felt backwards to me.

Also, when we were in Australia, we were staying with some friends of my friend. They lived right on the Swan River and we would sit and watch the beautiful black Tasmanian swans floating by on the river. Once, I suddenly had a flash that I had been there before! Then I finally found later on that some of my grandmother's family had definitely been down to Australia and over to the country of Ivory Coast in Africa and back to Virginia with a labor force for the colonies.[7]

After I told my sister about the information I had recently come in contact with, she sent me a copy of some hand written papers that she had gotten from my grandmother. I found out that those papers had been copied by my great-aunt, Elizabeth. She copied this bit of family history from the London Library when she was there on a visit. One document shows that Admiral William Boddie of the Royal Navy had fought against the Spanish Armada in 1585.

One of his descendants, another William Boddie, had been given lands every time he had brought colonists to the Province of Virginia, as it was referred to when it was first colonized. Later, it was referred to as the Colony of Virginia. He and his crew had delivered 136 persons there in three different voyages. In all, Boddie was given, by a Lord Mildmay, in total for his services to the crown, over 8,000 acres of land, in Isle of Wight county Virginia, in 1645.[8]

All of that granted land was, however, taken back by government and sold after the First World War in the 1930s to help pay for the war efforts in Europe. I was told by my aunt Hester her mother (my grandmother) received a payment of $8,000.00, in US funds for that 8,000 acres that had been granted her family. My only response to that information was, "Not bad; a dollar an acre."

The Boddie family, I found, was descended from roots in Denmark, the Orkney Islands, Isle of Man, Isle of Wight, Normandy and Anglesey Isle, in North Wales. I found at a later time, the Boddie name goes far back in the Welsh family histories.

Later I discovered on the Internet that the Boddie family line goes all the way back to Charlemagne and further. I have also discovered that King John and ten of the members that signed the famous English document, *The Magna Carta*, were related to my grandmother's family. I was not aware of this until I had my dreams and started doing research on my family history. The Boddies and the Pagets had both served in the Confederacy, all over the south, in the American Civil War in the 1860s.

The dream I had in November of 1994 was about my ancestors from Europe. I still don't know why I would have had these particular dreams. I didn't know anything about my family roots at that time. The only thing I can figure is, as I grew older, I began to want to know where the people in my families had come from. I was more interested than ever and wanted to know more about my past. Well I'll tell you, I got more than I was looking for. Since having that first dream, I've asked myself, over and over, *How did this happen?* All I could come up with at that time was the old saying: "Be careful what you wish for."

As a child, I always wondered if we might be related to some of the Native American people as well. I had a secret wish to be a part of those people somehow. Once when I was visiting my dad's family I was sitting with my grandmother and we were just talking. Finally, I got up nerve enough to ask her if my grandad was part native American. She quietly put down her cup of tea and turned to face me. I didn't know what to expect but then she said, "Yes, his mother was full-blood Cherokee from West Virginia. That means your grandad is half Cherokee. Your great-grandfather, Henry, married a woman whose name was Elizabeth Boggass." She had been taken in by a

French trapper family in West Virginia when she worked her way back there after having walked all the way to Oklahoma and found her way back to West Virginia. I was so excited but Grandma said for me to keep that to myself and I promised her I would. Recently, my sister did some research on that marriage and found a copy of the marriage certificate. It showed the names of my great-grandfather and my great-grandmother. Henry was registered as being white but it also showed Elizabeth was white as well. I discovered later that was normal practice in those days. I have reason to believe now that both my great-grandmother, on my father's side and my great-grandfather on my mother's side, separately took part in what was called the Long March, or Trail of Tears, during the presidency of Andrew Jackson under what was documented as the Indian Removal Act.[9]

My aunt Ruby, my mom's older sister, told me once that their father, William Pruitt, was born during the Long March and his mother was Cherokee and his father was Blackfoot. She also said that when her father, William Pruett, came back to North Carolina, his mother along with his father's Blackfoot family came back with him. Many Cherokee people where sent to Oklahoma on this forced march of relocation. My ancestors would have been taken from West Virginia and North Carolina, sometime in the 1830s. Some of them found their way back from Oklahoma and hid away in the mountains of the South.[10]

I asked my grandmother about her family background. Her name was Ellen Boddie. She told me her family names in Wales were Boddie and Rhys ap Thomas. My grandmother was petite; she only stood four foot eight inches tall. She said she had been born in Cardiff, Wales. Her family were sailors and owned sailing ships, as I have mentioned. She explained that they had lived in Portsmouth because that's where her family sailed out of as their home port. She said they had lost a lot of members of their family in storms at sea. Her people had been a part of bringing colonists to the eastern seaboard of the US, from Delaware to Georgia.

She told me about a hundred acres in the mountains at a place that was called Stapleton, Virginia. It was situated above the James River near Appomattox Court House. That was the place where

General Lee had supposedly surrendered to General Grant, thus ending the American Civil War.[11]

A Lord Stapleton had given that land to her family, in the early 1600s. My great aunt Elizabeth ended up with that place but I don't know what finally happened to it. That Stapleton name always rang a bell with me somehow. I did find the family name Stapleton-Cotton from the 1800s in my family tree. I always loved going there to be in the mountains and visit my aunt and uncle. As I got older, I wanted to know more about the history of that place but I never pursued it any further.[12]

When my uncle returned from the Second World War, the first thing he wanted to do was get away to a place that was quiet. So he headed up into the Blue Ridge Mountains, to the old Stapleton place. My uncle Dave could do a lot of things. He had learned how to build, so he went and built a new cabin on the old homestead.

I found out later on that he could play guitar and sing. I had never gotten to experience that part of him. Once, before he went to the war, he was living at the old home place in Lynchburg. While he was there, he started up his own radio station and was playing and singing on the air. He was doing fine, entertaining the mountain folk in that part of Virginia, until the Feds came in and shut him down! Shortly after that, he left to go to the army and fought in the South Pacific.

In the summers, I would go up there to stay with my aunt and uncle. I loved being in the mountains and going fishing and sneaking a ripe watermelon from a farmer's field and breaking it open right on the river bank and eating it. I also remember seeing the graves and the very old tombstones of some of my ancestors there.

A short time after I started collecting bits and pieces of my family history, to my amazement the Stapleton name came to the foreground again. Only this time, I was able to find out how far back in my family that name goes and how my past is connected to it. A couple of years ago, I was browsing around, once again, in a small secondhand bookstore and I came upon a thin little book, only 115 pages. I didn't realize at that time, that this book contained information that would change my life. This was truly an historian's dream!

The book I had found was entitled *The Knights of the Garter, 1348–1939*. It was researched and written by Edmond Fellowes and published by The Society for Promoting Christian Knowledge in 1939 in the UK. This research covers a time period from 1348 to 1939. I began going through this little jewel of a book. I was so proud of myself for having found it. Among the names in that publication, I came upon my own family name. As I mentioned before, I found a William Paget, who had been a privy councilor to Henry VIII. I couldn't believe what I was seeing.

Then I came upon another surprise. Lord Miles Stapleton, who was one of the founders of the Order of the Garter in 1348, was an ancestor of the same Lord Stapleton who granted my grandmother's family a hundred acres of land in the mountains in Virginia in the early 1600s, for bringing colonists there from England.

I was so delighted to find out where that name had come from. I began to realize then that I was slowly piecing the puzzle of my family history together and I started feeling good about that. It seemed to be coming to me in waves but all this history seemed to have a natural progression. I realized at this time in my research why these dreams had come to me. I believe it was to help me open up those channels to find out something that was important for me to know about my personal history.[13]

CHAPTER FIVE
Recorded History In Dream One

The first dream had taken place at Sudeley Castle near Winchcomb, Gloucestershire, close to the border of Wales and England. The focus of this dream was a woman named Lady Eleanor Butler née Talbot who would receive a secret visit from her only son whose father was Edward IV, the King of England. I now have reason to believe this was in May 1468. As I have already mentioned, the name of her son was Edward de Wigmore. In these dreams, he had been adopted by his mother's best friend, a woman by the name of Jane de Wigmore.[1]

In the most recent research I have done, I have now discovered that much of the information I received through the dreams is in the recorded history of the UK. I was able to find out what some of the family names, places and dates were, and why they were included in these dreams. I could not see how there could be so many precise details and also have them matching times of actual historical events, or at least close.

One of my first conclusions was that the events I found myself involved with in these dreams must have really happened in some past life. Their imprint was so clear and realistic, but it didn't seem to be in a logical order within the actual written history that I had researched. I don't believe these were just dreams of random events. These dreams have helped me find, and are still helping me find and understand, what my personal historical background was made up of. I had never heard of most of the characters and places I experienced in them.

I had never been inside an ancient castle but I would now experience being inside three of them in the context of these dreams. In that experience I had been able to mentally record what the floor plans of Sudeley Castle looked like. It is still a mystery for me to have been able to know what de Wigmore Castle's floor plan looked like, never having been there in my lifetime. That castle was partially razed by King Edward's troops when they left there to go to London. Edward did not want his enemy forces to use that castle as their fortress.

Young Edward was only an infant when he was first taken there. As soon as he had arrived there, everyone had to leave. Edward IV was on his way to find him and have him killed, as he may have tried to challenge his kingship someday. Jane de Wigmore and the FitzOsberne clan were quickly being approached by Edward IV's small army with sinister intents.

It took me a long time after the dreams were finished to draw the floor plans of these two castles from my recollections of them. I've included those floor plans for Sudeley and de Wigmore Castles in my author's documents. I had never been to see these named castles, nor had I seen any previous pictures or drawings of either of them. I had purposely waited until I had my drawings of these castles finished before I approached my contact in the UK, to receive a copy of the an original floor plan of Sudeley Castle.[2] I was very surprised and happy to see how close to the Sudeley Castle floor plans I had come with my drawing. I haven't found a good floor plan for de Wigmore Castle yet but I have composed a floor plan for that castle from an image I had from the dreams. Over the centuries, de Wigmore Castle has suffered much destruction from various political factions and the wear of time.

I decided that sometime in the near future I would like to go and visit these castles. I wrote to a place I thought might know something about the history of de Wigmore Castle. It had been built in the 11th century. I contacted an establishment in the Village of Wigmore and the proprietor wrote me this note in August of 2010:

"Thank you for your letter about Wigmore Castle. It is possible to reach the castle grounds after a walk through a managed forest. The castle can be reached via a shorter path that runs from the church in Wigmore Village. The castle ruins are open and available for visit all the time. However, you should be aware that the site does not have any visitor facilities or staff.

I've done a quick search on the name "de Wigmore" and found that it was an addition to the title of Roger Mortimer, the second Baron Mortimer of Wigmore c. 1306. The addition came after the accession of Edward II. It may be that your "de Wigmore" heritage links you to the Mortimer family. Records available on-line show the first recorded use of the name de Wigmore was at the church in Gloucestershire in 1239. Edward Plantagenet, King Edward IV, supposedly gave his male child the name Edward de Wigmore. The child supposedly died in infancy. It may therefore be that the name de Wigmore has a more complex origin than a simple relation to the castle in Wigmore."

After speaking with some of the local residents in Wigmore Village, I was informed that de Wigmore Castle had been acquired in 1996 and that, after three years of work costing one million pounds, the castle looked like it had for the last 200 years. The castle itself still seemed to be buried down about 25 feet. Apparently, the people who now own it want the area to be left in a natural state.

All I could think about was that is where my horse tunnels were located on the floor plans I had drawn from my dreams. The horse tunnels ran crossway of the castle and they were twelve feet wide. They ran east, out the back into the forest and west down the front on the ridge and came out in a bush area down the hill. I can still picture all of these details in my mind. I would just like to see it in real life and spend some time with it to see how close I came in drawing its layout.[3]

When I discovered the name of Lady Eleanor for the first time, I couldn't contain myself. Finding her in the actual history after dreaming about her has been one of the main highlights of this project. If I hadn't found her when I did, I may not have been able to have kept going on this mammoth task I had set out to complete.[4]

Lady Eleanor Butler née Talbot was a member of one of the three Talbot families which I have researched. Eleanor's family were known in the political circles in England, Ireland and Wales, as the Earls of Shrewsbury. In 1450, she had married a Sir Thomas Boteler (Butler). He was the son and heir of Ralph Boteler, who became Lord Sudeley and had rebuilt Sudeley Castle, almost to what it had been designed as in the 11th century.[5]

In 1459–60, Sir Thomas Butler and Owain Rhys-Jones, the husband of Jane de Wigmore, were both killed, according to my dreams and research, fighting with Henry VI's Lancastrian forces against Edward IV's Yorkist army. These battles were part of what was better known as the War of the Roses. This war was made up of two factions. The Yorkists, who were represented by the white rose, and the Lancastrians who were represented by the red rose. Sir John Grey, who was married to Elizabeth Woodville, was in command of Henry VI's cavalry and was killed at the Battle of St. Albans in 1461. This is the same Elizabeth that Edward IV supposedly secretly married in 1464, after having married Lady Eleanor Butler in 1461. I realize I am speculating here, but I began to see a pattern forming. Edward seemed to want to get rid of certain prominent Lancastrian men and it was perhaps done on the battlefield so it didn't look like murder. When Lady Eleanor married Sir Thomas Butler, Lord Sudeley had given them Sudeley Castle and two manor houses. They lived at Sudeley for ten years before Thomas died in battle, fighting Edward's Yorkists. Eleanor was then informed that she no longer had legal possession of Sudeley Castle or the two manor houses. Edward IV had taken possession of it all.

As one version of that story goes, Lord Sudeley had transferred two manor houses and Sudeley Castle in Warwickshire to his son on his marriage to Lady Eleanor, but had failed to obtain the King's permission for the transfer of title. Then Edward IV took over those properties. Eleanor asked Edward for their return to her. Edward was said to have given the properties back to Lady Eleanor, as she had requested, in early 1461.[6]

Another account of this same issue I found was that Edward IV wanted Sudeley Castle and in the 1460s he brought charges of treason against Ralph Boteler, Lord Sudeley. Sudeley Castle had been in the Boteler family since the early 11th century. Boteler had been a friend and patron of Henry VI. Lord Sudeley was then removed from the property and was not heard from again.[7]

In my documents at the end of this book, I have included a copy of the history of the owners of Sudeley Castle, which I received from David Ross at Britain Express in Cheltenham, Gloucestshire, UK. This information does not mention Lady Eleanor, or Sir Thomas Butler, ever owning Sudeley Castle or the two manor houses. In that same document however, it shows ownership passing from Edward IV to his brother, Richard, Duke of Gloucester in 1469. From what I have studied about this matter so far, I believe Sudeley Castle was never given back to Lady Eleanor. I believe she died under house arrest by Edward IV, in her own castle in 1468.[8]

Another strange issue here was when Lady Eleanor went to see Edward in 1461, to get her properties re-issued to her, Edward then proposed marriage to her. It was recorded that they were married in what was referred to as a "precontract marriage." Some historians did not agree totally with there ever being a precontract marriage between Edward and Eleanor. Even so, it was not considered to be a legal marriage.[9]

I have now found confirmation that shortly after Lady Eleanor and Edward were married, she became pregnant and there was a male child born to them. I then found other information that stated there was a male child born to Edward IV Plantagenet and Eleanor Talbot. Then it has been claimed that this same male child was born illegitimately in about 1467 and died in infancy.[10]

I found other information that had been made public in the mid-1600s by the fine British historian Sir George Buck, that explained that Edward IV and Lady Eleanor had a male child born to them. The child's name was known as Edward de Wigmore. The most important aspect of this information was that it explained that this son did not die in infancy as all the records that I had researched had stated. This young child was said to have been an ancestor of a Richard Wigmore who had worked in Elizabeth I's government. I believe King Edward IV, King Richard III and King Henry VII wanted everyone to believe this child had died in infancy because then that whole issue could just be left out of the public mind and out of the history.

A book I found in a used bookstore, *The Knights of the Garter, 1348–1939* by Edmond H. Fellowes, stated "1475(214) Edward (Plantagenet) Prince of Wales. Afterwards Edward V, King of England. Murdered with his brother Richard of Shrewsbury, and Duke of York, in the Tower of London."

The above date 1475 shows when Edward V (who was next in line to be King of England in April 1483, after his father's death) was registered in the Order of the Garter, along with his brother Richard of Shrewsbury. The word "afterwards" signifies the date, June 1483, when their uncle Richard III took his two nephews to the Tower of London.[11]

If this piece of history is true, it seems to me that many young males in royal families were in danger of being killed off before they could become kings. Just take a good look at Edward IV's ancestral line and you will see what I mean. Shakespeare was not joking in his play, *Hamlet*, when he says, "Get thee to a nunnery." This was a warning for young females of royal families. This was a warning for young males as well. Many children of these families died in infancy or did not live long.

In my research, I found it was believed by some British historians that Lady Eleanor died in 1468 at the Church of the Carmelite Order in Norwich. From the viewpoint of my dreams, I didn't believe Lady Eleanor died anywhere but in that bastille tower at Sudeley Castle.

I wanted to know what the true story was on this issue so I wrote a letter to the Carmelite Church in Norwich, UK. I asked if they had any record of a Lady Eleanor Talbot-Butler having been at their church in c1468 and birthing a male child and both dying and being buried there about that same year. The Carmelite Church kindly wrote me back and indicated they had no record of a Lady Eleanor Talbot-Butler or her infant son ever having been there. They did not die, nor were they buried, there. Even though they were receiving women in their church at Norwich by that time, neither Lady Eleanor nor her male child seem to have ever been resident there.[12]

I have seen information that said Lady Eleanor was buried at the Gray Friars Church in UK., the same as Richard III. When they might have been buried there is not certain. I don't believe that the foregoing statement concerning Lady Eleanor is true. In my dreams, Lady Eleanor was buried in the north-west garden of Sudeley Castle, right below the dungeon tower where young Edward had visited her. She spent her last months there before she passed away.

In my first dream, Lady Eleanor was languishing in that upstairs chamber where young Edward had met and talked with her for his first and only time. Shortly afterwards she had died.

For some of my research for this project I happened to read a publication on the life and career of Edward IV. In that whole book I didn't find any information about Lady Eleanor being married to Edward IV. However, there was information about Edward's marriage to Elizabeth Woodville in 1464. I did happen to see a footnote in that same publication, however, that stated Sudeley Castle had been granted to Edward's brother Richard, Duke of Gloucester who became Richard III. The two manor houses were given by Edward IV to court favorites in 1467.[13]

By way of review here, I want to mention that Lady Eleanor's short life was filled with hardship and grief. When she was only eighteen years old, she lost her father, Sir John Talbot, 1st Earl of Shrewsbury. He was killed while supporting the Lancastrian cause backing King Henry VI in France. In 1460 she lost her dear brother, Sir John Talbot, the 2nd Earl of Shrewsbury, in the Battle of Northampton, again fighting for Henry VI. In 1460, she endured the loss in battle of her husband, Sir Thomas Butler, whom she loved dearly and had been with for eleven years. Then there was supposedly the arrest and disappearance of her father-in-law, Ralph Boteler, Lord Sudeley. She did not know what finally happened to him. Then she lost the estates that she and Thomas had been given by Lord Sudeley. Edward IV confiscated the property namely, Sudeley Castle and two manor houses that were supposed to go to Lady Eleanor after she had lost her husband. Sudeley was then granted to Edward's brother, Richard, Duke of Gloucester in 1467.[14]

I believe Lady Eleanor died of starvation and cruelty while chained to the wall in an upstairs chamber of Sudeley Castle sometime c1468. Oddly enough, after changing hands many times, Sudeley became the property of Henry VII who had married Edward IV's daughter, Elizabeth of York. They were first cousins and were both related to Edward III. He then passed it on to his son, Henry VIII.

My ancestor, William Paget, along with his cohort, William Parr, would have spent a lot of hours at Sudeley Castle. They were both privy counselors to Henry VIII and were always there for functions of the government and to counsel King Henry.

I just want to note here an issue I found with the research that I had completed concerning the life of Lady Eleanor. Historians who mention her do not question why Eleanor would even consider marrying a man, Edward IV, who had already left her life in shambles. That question puzzled me until I was almost to the end of this story. Then I finally realized why she may have agreed to marry him. I discuss my reasons why I think Eleanor did marry Edward IV of her own volition in chapter fifteen.

CHAPTER SIX

Dream Two: The Dream Of Mount Snowdon

I had dream two in December of 1994. As I have explained before, this second dream was a shock and surprise because I knew now these dreams were an event I was meant to witness. I knew this was a very serious milestone in my life that I was to take part in. The historical time period of this dream was in May of 1461, the same time period as in dream one. This dream, as I see it, was a fragment of the first dream. I was now paying closer attention to the details because I was becoming more familiar with the characters and the settings. By the time this dream came about, I had time to collect enough historical information to study. From my studies I found enough factual material to realize I was on a good parallel course with the first dream. I felt more confident now and welcomed the second dream and put away my feelings of doubt and dread. I knew I was witnessing some sort of mental phenomenon which I had never experienced before.

The main thing I realized when the second dream began to occur was that I still had reservations I wanted to keep in place until I could prove these dreams had root in the actual history of that time. I felt this would give me some kind of mental protection, in case I became overloaded with information I might not be able to handle. I was fairly certain now, this first dream wasn't just a random event. As I recall, I still had a slight fear edge but my excitement seemed to keep any fear under control. I realized I didn't want my emotions to run wild and perhaps cause me to miss some of the key details being offered in these dreams. I didn't have to create any of this information; it was there for me to use or not to use.

The whole presentation in this second dream had an almost identical format as dream one. It started out to be a normal dream. I didn't wake up in a total panic this time. I seemed to know what to expect. I felt I had enough familiarity now with this kind of dreaming from my experience in the first dream, and I could guide myself through this one with more ease.

I welcomed this dream because I thought I might be able to answer some of the questions I noted from the first dream. I became excited because I began to think I could make these dreams work for me. I believed strongly now that they had something to say exclusively to me. My ego responded like a herd of wild horses. At first when I knew this second dream was underway, I had to quickly caution myself to be careful recording this dream and not let my ego cloud my vision. I knew I needed to pay very close attention to what was about to unfold. I didn't want to have any guesswork or preconceptions of what that would be. When I first realized I was dreaming, I felt I was being harassed but that didn't last long and I began to think I was privileged to be able to witness this happening, whatever its purpose may be.

To my amazement, in this second dream I did receive a lot of answers to questions I had already developed from the beginning of this whole episode. I felt from then on, I didn't know how many more of these dreams there would be. All I wanted to do at that moment was to concentrate only on what was about to happen. This time I felt more prepared emotionally. I didn't just throw caution to the wind but I didn't want to be so overly cautious that I couldn't grasp what the main information was that would be given. I had to tell myself to relax enough to remain open-minded. I thought if I could get some answers to the questions that were occurring from the information I had already received, then that is what I wanted. I believed the data I was seeing and hearing was not prescribed by anyone. I believed this was the raw material and it was for me to do with as I saw fit.

At the beginning of this dream, I just wanted to totally absorb the information as it came to me, with no idea or thought about what to do with it afterwards. In a spiritual sense, I thought if there were going to be more of these dreams, I wanted to experience them as meditations, without any expectations. As time passed, that idea didn't hold up well when I saw how much information there was written about this period of history. I began to want to use a method to short cut some of this information at least. Unknowingly, I was already aware of most of the characters I would be coming in contact with until the duration of these dreams. Some people might say I was just programming my own dreams, or I was telling my sub-conscious mind what I wanted to see. This was possible to a point, I suppose. I think we all want to see things the way we want them to be. That is why we become disappointed when our dreams don't turn out the way we think they should.

I could feel myself relax a little more in this dream, finally. I realized at the end of this series of dreams, I had even made some mentally strong attachments with some of the people I met in them. Almost every time I read over this manuscript, even after working on it for so long, there are scenes with Eleanor or with Jane which caused me to feel extremely emotional. I have felt my emotions were at a peak all the way through this whole writing. I was so moved by this dream experience that I took that as a sign that I must be interacting with people I had definitely interacted with in some time or dimension before.

In the second dream, Jane de Wigmore and her people had gotten word that Edward and his army were on their way to de Wigmore Castle, fighting their battles as they went. Jane's people, who had become young Edward's people as well, had packed everything they could. Jane and young Edward, on a horse together, left their beautiful old castle, not knowing if they would ever see it again.

They hadn't waited for Edward IV and his army to show up and confront them. Lady Eleanor had already warned them to get out, when she knew Edward was on his way there. He was going there to find young Edward and do away with him so he couldn't claim his royal rights for kingship. Edward's new young son was now surrounded by people of the old Lancastrian politic who would become known in the English political history as the Tudors.

Jane had always kept her family places that were originally built by her ancient ancestor, Earl William FitzOsberne, who was once the first Earl of Hereford. Both of these families had come to Wales when King William I had come to England in 1066. The Welsh never liked either family. The FitzOsberne clan traditionally looked after the de Wigmores. I have recently found information that claims the FitzOsberne clan was related to King William I.[1]

Aside from de Wigmore Castle, there was an old home castle, which was hidden away on Mount Snowdon. Earl William had built both places. These places had been their traditional homes for many centuries. Both of them had first been made out of big wooden timbers. Over many years they were finally built up of beautifully laid stone. As a family for generations, the de Wigmores always knew they could go to Mount Snowdon and be safe. In the dreams, young Edward was to grow up there. That place served them all very well as they all knew it could in times to come.

In dream two, Jane explained to young Edward about their trip to live on Mount Snowdon. He never suspected that Jane wasn't his real mother. He wouldn't know all this until he took that trip by horseback, in these dreams, to meet his birth mother at Sudeley Castle. That would be the only time he would remember seeing Lady Eleanor and spending a few precious moments with her, before she passed away. He was always glad he got to know the whole story of his early life. He was surrounded by people, who took him, raised, loved and respected him as one of their own. Jane was the only mother he had ever known, up until his meeting with his birth mother. He always wanted to stay close to where Jane was. He was with her when she passed away. He had grown to love her very much.

Jane was buried in the clan cemetery near de Wigmore Castle. Young Edward, always made it a point to look after her grave site and when no one was staying at Sudeley, he would go over and work around there. In these dreams, Jane's baby boy, Lars or (Larson) and Lady Eleanor were both buried in that same garden at Sudeley Castle.

Lars' dying at birth had allowed Eleanor to have him buried in the north-west garden just below the dungeon tower, where her life would end. By giving young Edward to Jane she thought there was a chance she could save his life. He also spent many hours musing over the life he had been able to live. He felt fortunate because of the way both Eleanor and Jane had been quick enough to work out the events that would save his life. He felt he had been very fortunate to have had two mothers who loved him so deeply.

In dream two, one morning in early April, Jane took him by the hand and led him with her out into the near garden, each with their own cup of tea. The sun was just coming up. Young Edward would never forget that setting. He felt the closest he had ever felt to her. He knew deep within himself, something big was about to happen that concerned the whole group of people he was now part of.

He felt a real uneasiness in his mind and body. He had always felt he had to become an adult before he was ready. He knew that was just the way times were he was living through. Jane and her clan had always made an effort to make him feel comfortable and welcome with them.

In the garden, Jane opened the conversation by telling him she was sending him away, temporarily, to stay with a man who had a farm. She explained to young Edward that he would ride his horse, Prince, with his Uncle Elborne, to a place near Cheltenham, England. This farm he was going to was located across the Severn River and then south.

The family he was going to stay with grew produce for the local castles. The man's name was Lorne Blackard. He had a son older than Edward and a younger daughter. Jane thought that Edward IV would be putting a lot of pressure on Wales, but she also knew he had to spend time on his home front. She thought young Edward would be better off, at least for a while, at the Cheltenham farm. Jane also said they were planning to move back into de Wigmore Castle in the near future at which time he could come back to his home with them again. She said she would send a message to him when the time came.

His last night at Snowdon seemed to go by quickly. He didn't remember dreaming that night. Morning seemed to come much too soon but at first light, Jane woke him. She had gotten up very early to make the morning meal and some food for his long ride. They finished up their parting meal. His mind seemed filled with many thoughts and emotions but he knew he had to move quickly. He went over to the kitchen area and Jane gave him a bag of supplies for their trip. As she handed him the bag, she hugged him and kissed him on the forehead. Young Edward took her by the hand and looked her in the eyes and told her he loved her very much; she then disappeared.

Then he ran and got his riding boots on and started hauling supplies out to the horse barn. His Uncle Elborne had Prince all saddled and ready to go. Edward gave him his bags and they were put in position on his packhorse. There was no one else around to say goodbye to. Then his uncle turned around and looked right at him and said, "All right son, mount up!" Young Edward would remember that feeling. He knew it was the start of a new segment of his life. He had such mixed feelings of excitement and a kind of apprehension. In a faint glimmer of sunrise, he took his last look around at what had been the only home he had known in his early years. He wanted to register the image of this place in his mind. He knew then, if he never got a chance to see it again, it would still be with him in his life forever.

He took his horse's reins in his hand, slid his foot into the stirrup and mounted him. He felt as though he had done this for many years. Maybe at some other time, somewhere else, he thought. He patted his horse on his mane and told him they were on their way on a long trip. Prince snorted his approval as they saw Elborne heading on his way, out of the horse barnyard. They followed him out of the home gate and moved on down the trail. Young Edward couldn't bring himself to look back.

Edward had ridden this trail with Prince many times before. Somehow, it seemed so different this time. He thought it was because of not knowing when, if ever, he would see that home place again. He took the trail for granted but when they started getting into new areas he didn't know anything about, he started feeling excited and paid closer attention. He studied the well-structured horse his uncle El rode. It was a light red gelding that was eight years old. His family always rode horses that blended well with their surroundings. This was just an unspoken trait of theirs, left over from their military background.

There were so many new evergreens and plants on this new trail. He hardly knew any of them by name. El encouraged him to know them all and know what they could be used for, medicinally and otherwise. The whole family knew the plants that grew around them and had used certain ones as medicines for centuries. So he could tell right away, this was going to be a learning experience for him, a whole new form of education. This reminded me, the author, of my grandfather teaching me herbal medicine when I was ten until I was thirteen years old. He got rid of asthma for me when I was ten.

El set the pace, a fairly quick one at that. Later on, when they stopped for a break, he took a map out of his bag that El had drawn for him. He wanted to see where they were on the trail. The map showed their starting point at Snowdon Mountain place and the rugged Cambrian Mountain trail going on to the headwaters of the Wye and Severn Rivers. The trail headed right through an opening of those two river systems. It was a good two whole days ride to a place called Builth Wells. That small town was situated right along the Wye River. They would stay with relatives of El's and feed their horses and themselves well. Then they would move to level ground when they approached the crossing of the Severn River.

While they were still traveling in the rugged Cambrian Mountains, they stopped to water the horses and themselves by a cool stream. As they sat by the stream, young Edward broke the silence with El by saying, "It's nice to be traveling in these mountains for the first time." El turned toward him and fixed him in his gaze and said, "Oh no lad, this isn't your first time. I packed you through here, on this same trail, when you were just a baby. We traveled through here in the winter. The snow was up to the horses' bellies. There was lots of wind and it was cold." Edward sat there in amazement, not because El had said that much but that it was hard for him to envision El bringing him through there on horseback when he was just a baby. Even so, he felt at home there and a deep sense of pride, as he listened to this tale for the first time.

They finally reached the place where they had to cross the English border. It was just getting dark and they knew they would soon be crossing the Severn River. Edward had to tell El he was scared out of his skin. El sensed he was getting worked up again because he knew he had to cross his first big river on horseback. El tried to calm him down and told him he knew a good place to cross and to just follow him. "You'll get used to it. If the water gets too deep, let the horse have its rein and he will swim if he has to. Just let him go where he feels good and he will do all the work for you."

They finally got to the river crossing and El followed the trail right down to the water's edge and kept on going. Edward followed along keeping an eye on El, to see if he was watching him. Then, he just let his horse, Prince, have his rein and he acted as though he had crossed this water a thousand times before. When they got to the other side they skirted around the town of Hereford and headed for the town of Cheltenham.

By the time they got across the Severn they had to make camp between Hereford and Cheltenham. El didn't want to have a fire at their camp that night, so they wouldn't call any extra attention to themselves. They had to take off their wet clothes and put on some dry ones. They slept dry and got a well deserved rest that night. They woke at "first light" and ate some food from the bag Jane had packed for them.

They didn't have any more big rivers to cross and Edward was excited to meet his new family. He knew he would be living there for awhile. Again they stayed on the outskirts of the town of Cheltenham and later got back onto the main trail. As they went on for a good ways from the town, El then turned off the main trail onto a smaller wagon road. They traveled a short way on that trail and came to a clearing. Then they saw a house over on the far edge of a clearing. Edward suddenly got very excited when he realized the whole place here was the farm he would be calling home for awhile.

There was smoke coming from the chimney of the farmhouse and as they got a little closer, a tall, stout man came out and greeted them. Right away he told them he was Lorne Blackard. They rode up close to the man and El introduced himself to him and they shook hands. After they climbed down off of their horses, Lorne approached them and said, "You must be Edward?" "Yes," he said, as they shook hands. He could tell this was a hardworking man by the feel of his hands. It was now getting on in the day and El explained to Lorne he wanted to get back home as soon as he could. They seemed to get along very well for having just met each other. It almost seemed as though they knew each other from somewhere before. Then they both started unloading the packhorse. El explained to Lorne that the gelding Edward was riding was his own horse and would it be all right to leave him there, so he would have his own mount. "By all means, we'll put him in that barnyard, until he settles in with the other horses," Lorne spoke up.

Then El explained to Lorne that the family didn't know when they would move back into de Wigmore, but they would get a note to Lorne and Edward when the time came. "I understand," Lorne replied. El came over to Edward and Lorne took his mount and moved on toward the barnyard as they said their goodbyes. El was not a sentimental person but he was very sincere. He said, "We love you lad and we will not forget you. You are part of our family now. Hopefully, in a short time we will come and get you and take you home." He bent down and gave him a hug. He did look at him but turned around quickly, got the lead for his packhorse and mounted his horse. As he rode away, he called goodbye to Lorne.

Young Edward enjoyed his life with Lorne and Lorne's caretakers, and they treated him as if he belonged there. He still missed Jane and he said good night to her every night before he went to sleep. He would fall asleep thinking about her and when he would be able to be with all of them again.

CHAPTER SEVEN
Dream Three: The Full Circle

Lorne laid in supplies at a lot of the castles around the area of his farm. Then, one day Lorne asked young Edward if he wanted to go with him to make a delivery to Sudeley Castle. So without much thinking about it, he said he would go, just to see some new country and to see that castle. At least, that's all he thought he was going for, but it turned out to be far more than he could have imagined.

When they arrived at Sudeley Castle and had come to a stop, Lorne turned to face him and spoke in a warning kind of voice. He said, "If anyone should ask your name, you tell them you are Henry Blackard, Lorne's son. You don't tell anyone your mom is Jane de Wigmore. You do not mention that name here. Do you understand?" Edward told him he did but he really couldn't understand why all of a sudden Lorne was acting so strange. He felt more frightened than anything else now. He felt totally confused.

Lorne tied up the horses to a hitching post near a side door and they walked into the main hall of a beautiful castle together. The servants, mostly women, moved quickly past them. They seemed too busy to notice their presence. That was just fine by young Edward. He was too awestruck to carry on a sensible conversation with anyone at that time. He just wanted to remain invisible.

Lorne stopped and told Edward to wait, right where he was, until he had finished delivering his order; he would come and get him when he was ready to go. Edward told him he would give him a hand moving in the supplies but he said no. Edward didn't know if he should have come along now or not. He felt misplaced and didn't know even where he should wait.

Women passed back and forth from the kitchen area through some big doors that led outside. He could see where they were all going and that they were taking large plates of food to tables outside on the large field in front of the castle. Because the servants moved so freely around him, that gave him mixed feelings of belonging and not belonging at the same time. It also gave him a feeling of not being present, at least not in the flesh.

Young Edward, began to feel he was becoming involved with this place, for some reason. It was as though he was watching a play. Then after he had calmed down some, he became interested in watching what he thought were the daily activities of a place such as this. He realized he was starting to enjoy himself a little more.

He felt as though nothing was expected of him here and he began to relax somewhat, with a feeling of no responsibilities. He was completely aware of all the activity that was taking place around him. There in the near distance, he could see men in combat armor riding large framed horses, the type used for battle. He knew this was a type of combat training because he had watched the FitzOsbernes on Mount Snowdon carrying on this type of military training. They had told him that he would be trained when he was older, in his teens.

The military men he watched walk past him were wearing very high leather boots, metal plating and they carried their metal helmets under their arms. Then he saw two men go past him very closely. They came so close, he could have reached out and touched them. Their metal armor glimmered in the sun as they walked past him and through the doors that opened onto the big front lawn.

What took him so strangely about those two men, who had walked so closely to him, was that he still had a feeling that maybe he didn't belong there. He suddenly began to feel out of place again when they walked by. He hadn't felt anything like that from any of the other men who had walked by, even though some of them had walked close to him as well.

He realized he had taken a special notice of those two men sub-consciously. They were the first two characters he had a surprisingly high amount of interest in at that place. He felt a sudden need to know who they were. He had a strong urge to follow them but he held back because he knew Lorne wouldn't like him moving around all over the place. Now, all of a sudden, he realized he was no longer watching someone else; he felt a strange feeling of being involved there for some reason and he didn't know why.

Edward soon lost sight of the soldiers in the bright sunlight and sort of forgot them for the moment. He thought perhaps Lorne could tell him who those two soldiers were if he could point them out to him later. Lorne knew who ran the castle and the people that came there on a regular basis. He had lived in that area all his life and had served them with his garden produce for many years. Young Edward didn't know then how much he would come to know of the soldiers and how much a part of the actual history of that era they were.

He tried to put these two men out of his thoughts but he realized it wasn't that easy. He realized he had instantly focused on them and tried not to draw too much attention to himself as they passed by. He didn't realize he could record so many details about them so quickly. One man was very tall. He was the taller and older of the two men. He had long red hair; he wasn't gray and he looked to be about forty years old. He seemed to be a trainer or bodyguard for the younger man. The smaller man was very young. It seemed he was only about fifteen years old or so and not as tall as the older man. With his helmet off and under his arm, his hair was dark red and shorter.

Try as he might not to have them notice him, as they passed by the taller man did turn and look directly at him. The younger man went on about his way, not focusing on him. They seemed more interested in getting back out to the activities in the field as though they were working on some kind of military training. What confused Edward about the younger of the two men was that he reminded him of a host. He had seen him, when he had first arrived there, in the kitchen area and the servants had all been bowing to him when he came into the room. It also seemed he was giving some kind of instructions to the kitchen help. He knew he was someone of high rank.

Edward was just starting to calm down from those two men going by him. Now he realized he was pacing around so he tried to stand still. He decided to go over and lean against one of the massive walls of the kitchen area. Just as he began to relax a little, suddenly he heard, or thought he was hearing, a high-pitched cry! This sound happened so quickly, he couldn't tell if it was coming from near or far away with an echo. Then he heard it again and again, at separate intervals. It was so high pitched he thought it had to be a young girl or a woman. It seemed that whoever was calling out was caught or stuck and was desperately crying out for help.

He seemed to be suddenly confronting two tasks at once. His whole attention seemed to be focused on this person who was crying upstairs. He was totally confused! He couldn't understand why no one was concerned about this person's cry for help. He seemed to be the only one, in that whole big place, who was concerned for this person who sounded in desperate need of assistance.

It took him a while to locate where the sound of this voice was coming from. The sound apparently was coming from right in front of where he was standing, at the top of a heavy granite staircase that ran against a high wall leading up to another level. He went over and counted, twenty-one stone stairs, and saw a small window in the thick stonewall at the top of the narrow stairwell. While he was standing there looking at those stairs, he heard a woman's voice for certain this time, and it was definitely coming from up those stairs.

Young Edward felt as though he was beginning to panic! His movements were uncertain. He wanted to run for help, so he ran into the kitchen area but no one was there. He turned and headed for the door where he had entered the castle. Suddenly, he stopped as he caught a glimpse of the women and men servants, who were all out on the lawn, serving food to the soldiers while they did their training. He began to swear out loud. Jane had always taught him that swearing was not good for the soul. He was shocked because no one was trying to offer any help to someone who was crying out for it.

At this point, young Edward no longer seemed to be an innocent by-stander. He was confused and overcome by the urge to get some-one's attention and go with them to help the person crying upstairs. He was held back by the thought too, that Lorne would be angry with him for not staying where he had told him to.

Suddenly, out of the midst of the bright sunshine from the door-way onto the fields, he spotted a tall man in armor plating, with his helmet under his arm. The light was bright toward him but he could see the outline of a male figure walking in what seemed to be in his direction. He could see a man's outline but he couldn't see his face.

He found himself feeling many feelings at once. All he could think of was his gladness for maybe getting someone's help for the person up-stairs. He wasn't thinking in his child's mind anymore. Now, he seemed to be able to think in an adult's mind, thinking more quickly than he ever had. When this man figure was almost to him, young Edward rushed up to him and in a loud, agitated voice, he asked the soldier for his help for the person crying out from upstairs. He knew the soldier could hear the same sound he was hearing because he was standing right in front him. Then, as this man bent down from his tall posture, Edward thought he better listen to what he was going to say to him. Then, he sud-denly caught a glimpse of the man's eyes and face. He knew instantly he should not have said anything to this man. Now he knew it was too late!

Then the tall man bent down even closer to him, as if someone might overhear what he was about to say. When his words reached young Edward's hearing, he suddenly felt so afraid, he thought he was going to be sick! The man then began to speak to him in a deep, threat-ening demeanor, as he said, "I want you to forget that person upstairs. You shall not go up there and if we should find you up there, you shall be dealt with in a very serious manner. Do you understand what I am saying to you, lad?"

Young Edward couldn't remember saying anything back to the sol-dier, but he did remember being asked his name, why he was there, and who he was there with. Then, he remembered when the man said, "All right then." He remembered seeing him turn, in one determined motion, and quickly move back outside, the way he had come in. All he could remember, when the soldier left, was hearing the clacking of his hard-heeled boots against the thick stone slab floor. As he walked away, he didn't look back, not even once, to see if his message had left its mark.

All young Edward knew at this point was that the soldier now knew who he was, or at least who he had told him he was. He was also aware that the man knew the woman, whoever she was, needed help upstairs. Young Edward felt physically jarred, when out of the fog he found himself in, he heard that same voice pleading again. The calling seemed different to him now. He didn't know if he was just hearing it differently because of his fright or if the tenor of the voice had some-how changed.

Now it was as if the person was calling to him explicitly for help! He thought at first that was just his imagination. He knew he was feeling extremely afraid for his young life. Yet strangely enough at the same time he had a feeling of solemn comfort. As a light misty fog cleared in his mind, he could see an image of himself that was from above looking down on him. He saw himself looking up, as though he was posing. What was so strange about this scene was that he seemed to be smiling, in a victorious type of expression.

Now, he began taking on a deep sense of bravery! This didn't seem to fit his frail body or mind. Still, he remembered feeling so odd he had to note it quickly. He felt excessively strong and ready as a warrior for battle and equal to the task at hand. By now, there weren't many servants or anyone else moving around this great hall in which he still found himself.

He suddenly caught himself wondering what had happened to Lorne. Then, when he couldn't find anyone to give him some kind of support, he began to feel his mood suddenly changing. He was wanting to run into the forest and hide and get away from this awful place! That dreadful sound that wouldn't go away, started making him think he was in over his head and there was nothing he could do about this situation.

Again, he found he was back to his old self and he just wanted to give up and run. Then, he couldn't decide which way to run. He was feeling helpless. He thought he could beat that feeling, but then he started crying and trying to hide it. He felt the most confused he had ever been in his short life.

He began to wonder what would happen if he just went up there to see if he could help that poor person. He thought nothing could make him as afraid as he already was. He felt he was getting used to the feeling of sudden fear or fear in general. He began to talk to himself, mumbling "What will I do when I get up there; will I find the door locked? How will I get it open? What will I do if that person is hurt?" All these calculating thoughts were running through his mind.

Suddenly, out of nowhere, came the sound of footsteps. This was all happening so fast, he didn't know how much he could go through before he just couldn't do this anymore. He quickly turned around to see a tall servant woman coming toward him. She was alone, as if she had planned it that way. He didn't know what he was in for now, as she kept coming right up to him. All he could think was, *Where is Lorne?* Under his breath he said, "Lorne got me into this; he's got to get me out of here, I can't do this anymore."

Unexpectedly, this servant woman, when she got up to him, reached out her hand and he was shocked by her kindness. He hesitatingly took up her offer. In a soft tone, as soft as her hand, she said, "I see you have been crying, but be brave for now, and this will be over soon." He didn't know whether to trust her kindness or not. To him in that moment it seemed to be in short supply there. "What was she talking about?" he asked himself. He was beginning to think this was a very strange place with a lot of strange people. The servant woman bent down to him, after she looked around to see if anyone was watching them. Then she said to him in a whisper, "Come with me; we don't have much time." There was no one around that he could see in this whole big hall. She walked him over to that granite stone staircase and she started giving him instructions as to what she wanted him to do. He suddenly thought about Lorne getting angry with him.

The servant woman, after she had made sure no one would see them, said, "Go up these stairs to the top. At the head of the landing there you will see a big door to a small room on the outside wall. The person you have heard crying is in that room. Go to the only door there and push up on the heavy handle and that will release the bar that holds the door closed. Then push the door open. The woman in that room desperately wants to see you, but you must hurry." He tried to talk but she told him to get going. She told him not to stay in there very long, only a few minutes. Her final warning was that if anyone found him in there with that woman, he would be under house arrest and could be killed for just talking to her.

Young Edward suddenly had wavering thoughts as to whether he even wanted to go up there at all now. But he brushed those thoughts aside quickly. All he could think at that moment was that this kind servant woman was putting her life on the line as well, just so he could try to help that poor person who was crying out from that room. All he could think was that if that servant woman was willing to risk her life to help that person up there, then so was he! The servant woman said, "When you come back down, come into the kitchen area and Lorne will be there waiting for you."

She had given Lorne a note she received. She said for him to ask him about it later, after they had left there. Edward started asking all kinds of questions but she just said there wasn't enough time. Then, she said, "Go now and all your questions will be answered by the time you come back from that room. Go quickly! Bless you! I'll pray for you to be safe."

Edward couldn't think; all he could do was what the servant woman had told him to do. He started stretching his tiny legs to go up those twenty-one stone stairs and see what awaited him there. He didn't know what he had to do with that person. He didn't get to ask any questions. He thought, at least, someone was concerned about who this person was and why they were crying. He felt a sudden flash of happiness that he had been asked to help. That seemed to mask his fear, for that moment.

As he was stretching his legs to make the next step, it occurred to him that he was crying. Through his tears, he was mumbling a little prayer to have someone look after him in all this. He was having a hard time believing this was happening. In what seemed to be some very quick minutes, he reached for the last stair, completely out of breath. Then, he turned and looked back down the stairs to see if anyone was watching him. He saw the big heavy door, the short hall and the high wall. This upstairs chamber seemed very small indeed.

He tried to catch his breath but he was so excited, he quickly went on with the instructions he had been given. Before he lifted the heavy iron bar up, he put his ear against the door, to see if he could hear anything. All was silent. He was being careful not to make any sound that could be heard downstairs. He knew the stairwell could magnify the sound in an echo downstairs. He reached for the iron bar and pulled it up as far as it would go. As he pushed up on it, he leaned against the door, with all the weight of his whole body. At that moment, he felt so small. He just hoped he had enough strength to carry out this mission. He felt he had already aged so much, from the time he met the woman downstairs until now. His last thought before pushing open the door was feeling that everything that was happening seemed to be in slow motion, like a dream.

Young Edward knew he was crossing some sort of threshold he had never crossed before. He also knew, that crossing it would mean his life would change forever. He felt, in his child's mind, he would never be the same person he was now, after he saw the person in that room and returned back downstairs. As his small hands grasped the thick door and his body pressed against it the door made a creaking sound as it slowly opened. There before him was a sight no child should see at any time. He stood frozen in a totally confused, almost mindless posture. He couldn't believe what he was seeing or if he was really seeing it. He felt his mind was trying to catch up with his body.

Right in front of him, in the bright daylight coming from the only window in the room, was standing a tall thin woman, with matted hair, as black as coal. She looked to be about thirty-five or forty years old.

She was dressed in rags; a dark brown sweater over a wool skirt and a ragged shirt. She was barefoot and was trembling as she fixed him in her stare. He couldn't see any source of heat in this chamber and it was cool in there except for a little bit of sun.

The stench in there was awful. She could not bathe and she looked as though no one had made any attempt to do anything for her, except place a little food in there. She barely had any water to drink, let alone to bathe with. Her movement was restricted because of a short chain that held her to the wall. The chain from the wall was hooked to thick leather bands that she wore on her thin little wrists. They were rubbed raw by the leather straps. Her bed was a straw mat on the bare stone floor. She had two ragged blankets that didn't look fit for a dog's bed. There were some bits of food scattered all over the room. Her toilet was a hole in the floor.

All he could do was stand there in total preoccupation with this rancid setting and this ghost-like figure of a woman. It was easy to understand now why she was calling out for help. She was definitely being held a prisoner, and starved to death at the same time. He wanted to know why. He suddenly wanted to know so much but yet he felt embarrassed to ask her to explain her situation. He still had a need to know what was happening. He had risked his life, and hers as well, to be there with her. It had to be important to both of them, he thought. He felt he had to get some answers but he didn't know where to start and there was so little time.

Young Edward didn't know how long he had already been there, but he knew he must try to get some answers and go very quickly. As he tried to move, to get something to happen, a thought over-came him. It was a musing of sorts, as he was so taken by the calm demeanor of this person and the expression on her face. It reminded him of a word he had heard used once by a man his Uncle Thorsen knew. The word the man used was "esperance." When he asked his uncle what that word meant, he explained that in the old French it meant hope or expectation. Then he told him, that in the Old Spanish, it meant "the spirit of the dead, among the living." Edward couldn't help thinking how that word was so fitting to describe the expres-sion this woman had on her face. She had such a look of hope and expectation. She seemed to be so calm but looked as though she was dying. *How could this be possible?* he asked himself. He turned away from her and considered running, but then he thought, *No, I'm here and I'm going to find out what I came here for and get out of this place for good.*

Finally, the woman broke the silence and spoke to him in a notice-able Irish accent that even he as a child could detect. She spoke in such a soft voice for a person in such a desperate situation as she was in. She then reached out her hand and said, "Please come and hold my hand, my son." His legs and feet felt as heavy as stone. He didn't know if he could walk to her, even if he wanted to. He didn't want to get so close that he would smell her but he felt he had to be kind to her and dismiss that idea for the moment.

Edward moved slowly over to her and placed his small hand in her slender, chapped hands. As she clasp his hand in both of hers, he felt so much love from her. There was a sudden explosion of emotion and they both began to weep. She took him, full in her arms, and held him there, as no one ever had, besides Jane. At that moment he felt more love than ever! For a moment, he forgot her matted black hair and the smell of the filth. He began to see her as an extremely beautiful woman with wavy black hair and bluish/green eyes that he felt could see right through him. Her magnetism was focused on him and he felt completely helpless! He thought she would never release her grasp. She gave him a feeling of a candidate for sainthood.

Finally, she released him from her arms but still held his left hand. Then she looked into his eyes and fixed him in her stare. She had his full attention and said, as he was wiping away his tears, "We must hurry; it is very dangerous for you to be here." He told her he had been well instructed of that.

She began, "I know I'm not going to live much longer so I wanted to see you and hold you in my arms and tell you these things." Edward had no idea what she was talking about. He began to think she was insane! He was frozen into position, waiting for her next words. He kept thinking, *Why is she taking so long?* He just wanted to get out of there. Now that he had seen she was chained up and there was nothing he could really do to help her, he just wanted to make a run for it, down those stairs and as far away from there as he could get.

She then said, "I am more concerned for your life than my own. I asked to have you brought here so I may tell you what I have to say to you. I had to wait until you were old enough to understand. I want you to keep this with you for always."

Finally he had enough, and in a burst of uncontrolled emotion, he said, "I can't take this anymore, who are you? Jane de Wigmore is my mom and I don't know who you are or how you know her or me or Lorne. My mom left me with Lorne, the man who brings the food supplies here. My mom has gone back to the old home place in Wales," he burst out in an almost blaming way. The woman then cautioned him to be as quiet as he could and that really angered him. He knew she was right. Then he said, "What is it you have to say to me? I just want you to say it so I can get out of here."

The woman then asked him to close the door. He had forgotten it was open. He walked over to the door and suddenly wanted to run and forget this whole thing. He turned back and faced her and said, "How do I know this isn't some kind of weird trick?" She spoke up right away and said, "No, my son!" Almost yelling, he exclaimed, "Don't call me that; I am not your son! My mom is Jane de Wigmore." The woman came back with, "Yes, you are my son, I am your mother, Lady Eleanor! I was married to Edward IV in a private ceremony. Edward IV is the King of England and I am the Queen of England, and you are my only son and you are a Prince!

"Jane de Wigmore, who is my best friend, is your adopted mom. She adopted you when she birthed her son, Larson, and he died of the fever soon after he was born. You were born at almost the same time he was. We, Jane and I, wanted to bury her baby here in the garden. Then I asked her to take you, so Edward wouldn't have you killed. Edward didn't want to have children with me, he just wanted his sons by Elizabeth to inherit his kingship.

"Edward wanted my estates and to hold me a prisoner here, as a slap in the face of my family. My husband, Sir Thomas Butler, gave the estates to me in his will. My husband and Jane's husband were killed by Yorkist troops on a trip into Wales to solicit more mercenary soldiers for the war. Edward had no choice but to keep me here as a prisoner because I know too much about him and his secrets.

"After Edward found out from one of his servants that Jane and I had exchanged babies, he went searching for you at de Wigmore Castle. When he arrived there with his army, the whole family, including you, were gone! Edward occupied de Wigmore Castle and fought battles from there. He won his battles and then went to London to be installed as the new king. He was aware that people had been living at de Wigmore, he had his army destroy as much of it as they could because he didn't want the opposing army to be able to use that castle as a fortress.

"Enough said, my son, we have risked your life to have you come here to see me. I shall remember you for the rest of my short life. I hope you shall remember me. I shall think of you often with much love, my precious son, Edward de Wigmore. Go quickly and carefully now. Godspeed, my Prince!"

When she called him her Prince, they both were in tears as they held each other in a final desperate embrace. Their hands slid away; they fixed each other in a final stare and said their forever goodbyes. Edward then turned, reached for that big door and went through the opening, not daring to look back. He closed that thick, heavy door. With the sound of the door latch still present in his mind, it was all he could do to stumble back down those cold stairs, almost falling at times, trying to wipe away his gushing tears. Now, he had to bear the sound, over and over again of the echo of metal on metal, of that iron bar falling into its holder and barring that door again, holding his mother a prisoner. He felt as though he was a prisoner about to die, and all he wanted to do was get out of there forever!

He couldn't tell how long he had been up there. With all the ground he and his mother had covered, it felt timeless. Whatever time it took, his whole personal history had suddenly run through his small little brain. He couldn't think about any logical thought. All he could feel was a kind of animal preservation to just get out of there and get totally away from these people.

When he had finally made it down to the main hall again, he checked to see if anybody was there. He couldn't see anyone around so he made a dash for the kitchen. No one was there or anywhere that he could see. Just at the peak of feeling trapped again, he ran out of the kitchen to head for the side door he had come in at. He suddenly ran into the woman who had helped him get up-stairs, almost colliding with her he was rushing so fast.

She bent down and took him by the hand. She knew he had gone through a trauma. She gave him a motherly hug and said, "Come on, I'll take you to where Lorne is waiting to take you back home."

They walked outside through the side door they had first come in at. As they got outside, Edward took a big breath of air. He felt as though he hadn't taken a deep breath for a long time. There were various people standing around, men and women socializing and some men were still out on their horses. As they strolled toward the out-buildings, he realized it was a small horse barn. Soon, he caught a glimpse of Lorne harnessing the horses beside the wagon. He felt a sudden relaxation of his whole being.

When they got to Lorne, he gave them a welcome hello and put his massive hand on his shoulder and said, "Are you ready to travel, lad?" He looked up at him and said, "I sure am." Lorne thanked the woman with a certain familiarity as though they had been friends for a long time. She had been so kind to young Edward he knew he wouldn't forget what all she had done to make this whole event happen. She had risked her own well being. As she stood with them there, young Edward said, "Would you please tell me your name." "I'm sorry, I thought you would have known each others names by now," Lorne said. "No, we didn't take that time yet," she said. "My name is Margaret Mitchell." As tears welled up in her eyes, she quickly said goodbye, turned around and was gone. Young Edward watched as she made her way through the grass of that field and was finally swallowed up by that massive building again. He knew this was a place he would never be able to put completely out of his mind.

Even though he felt a little safer now being back with Lorne again and having been helped by such a kind person as Margaret, he was still harboring a strong dislike for this whole place. He felt it had a strong magnetic hold not only on him, but his mother as well. He felt a great sense of frustration and guilt in knowing he would be free to go with Lorne in the wagon with the horses. He also knew he didn't have to ever see this place or be here again. He couldn't cleanse his thoughts of the fact that his birth mother was a prisoner here inside this place. He also knew she would lose her life here, from starvation and a broken heart, at the hands of those few awful people.

He felt a very strong hatred for all those rich bastards that went on having their fun and frolicking and never showed any sign of concern about his mother's painful suffering and her tragic cries for help. He didn't realize that at such a young age he was capable of hating so much. Finally, his musings came to a halt, when he heard Lorne's voice saying, "It's time to go." He felt a quickening in his heart and mind. He was never so glad to leave a place in his life, as he was to leave this place now.

As he left Sudeley Castle, he didn't look back, not even once. He wanted to pretend it was just a dream, and it didn't even happen, but he knew it had happened and it was still happening, even though he was leaving. He had no way of knowing how long his mother would be forced to suffer there. He thought about where they would finally bury her. His saddest thought was that he was leaving and he couldn't do anything to stop these vicious people from treating his mother the way they had and still were. He knew his visit there didn't mean anything to them. After he had time to consider the experience he had just had, he surprised himself with the idea that he was suddenly relating to her as his real mother and that he was already trying to defend her.

When at last the team of horses set their pace for the trip home, the only home he knew right then, he broke down and cried uncontrollable tears. Lorne quickly took both sets of reins in his left hand and then he placed his right hand around Edwards tiny shoulder and said, "It's good to let it all go and get shut of it, then you'll feel a lot better. It's not your fault, lad." He looked up at him through his tears and mumbled, "How can people be so cruel and mean? What are they driven by; what causes them to treat her like that? It's almost as though they enjoy watching people suffer. That's the meanest thing I've ever seen in my life."

Lorne came back to try to answer his questions and said, "I don't know why people do the things they do. I'm just a simple man, trying to live my life. Just remember, I'll be your friend and you've got Jane as your adopted mom. You have already told me that she loves you as much as her own flesh and blood son. You have to learn to let the hatred go, because if you don't and you keep it alive, it will come to spoil your soul. If you keep the hatred you feel for certain people at Sudeley inside you, soon it could ruin you and you won't be able to love anyone anymore. We as humans can't always figure out why things happen in our lives, the way they do. Believe me, I know what you are going through right now."

Edward suddenly responded to Lorne, with heat, and spouted back, "No you don't! You've never gone through any of this I'm going through now. This is the worst thing anybody my age could have to go through!"

"I don't believe degrees of sadness are determined by age. Sadness is sadness; no matter what age you are when it comes to you. It doesn't pick and choose who it attacks, it just shows up," Lorne said.

Then, Lorne shocked him by turning to face him and in a quivering voice he said with conviction, "Believe me, I do know!" Edward was caught off guard by the sound of his voice. He turned and faced him so he could see his expression and when he did finally face him, he could see tears running down his face. Right away, he thought he would seize the moment and make a smart remark, "Oh! I didn't know you could cry." Lorne came back with, "Well, what did you think, I wasn't human?" "No," he said, "it just surprised me. Would you tell me what happened to you?"

Wiping his tears away, Lorne began to tell young Edward his tale. "Five years ago, I was traveling over to the Village of Hereford. It was in the spring time. I had the Severn River change my life for me, forever. I had my wife Rose and my son, Harry." Edward interrupted him with, "I didn't know you had a wife or another son. I thought the people I met at the farm were your son and daughter." Lorne came back with, "No, they are my neighbours' children. They come and look after the farm when I go away.

"I took the wagon and horses to the best place I had always crossed in *freshet* and I prepared to cross. We were taking a load of supplies up to Goodrich Castle, located up on the Wye River. We all three, were riding on the front board of the wagon. My son Harry was about as old as you and before we tried to cross, I covered everything I could in the bed of the wagon. Then Harry went down onto the floor of the wagon. I tied a piece of rope around the seat board, so we would all have something to hold on to, in case things got too rough in the water.

"We all said a prayer together as we always did and asked the creator to protect us as we crossed the river. Then we started into the river. The water was moving faster than I had ever seen it. People in that area used that crossing a lot. We were in mid-stream and were doing all right. The horses and wagon were still touching the bottom of the river. Suddenly, when I looked back up the river, I spotted an uprooted oak tree in the main river current, coming right at us. I couldn't turn the horses enough to get out of its way, so I had to wipe the team to get out of the tree's pathway. Now my wife was screaming for me to save them. I can still hear her sometimes when I'm asleep and I wake up. My son was too afraid to speak. He held on as long and tight as he could.

"Then, that whole oak tree, came crashing over us and trapped us under it. I had to let go the reins. The horses were caught under the biggest limbs. When I saw the horses go under the current I knew I couldn't reach the traces to unchain them from the wagon. I tried to free my wife and my son but they were both trapped in the floor of the wagon. We were all struggling to get out of the wagon, when another oak tree, a smaller one, smashed into the side of the wagon and dragged me out. I then lost my grip and was swept away to the shore we were crossing to. I stood up in the shallows not far from shore. I found myself holding onto a tree limb on the bank, just in time to see that big oak carry my family, my horses, my wagon and all the supplies down the Severn River.

"I couldn't believe this was happening to me. I had done this all my life. This was the only life I knew; now it was all gone. I was broken and bloody and exhausted mentally and physically. I pulled myself up on the bank and I could still see the big tree floating down the river. I ran as fast as I could go through the bush, not to lose sight of that tree going down the river. The big tree finally caught on a fallen tree on the shore at the bend in the river. All I could think about was being able to go and save Rose and Harry.

"When I got to the logjam, I was calling as loud as I could but the rush of the water blocked the sound of my calling. I worked my way out to the oak they were trapped under. Suddenly I saw the dead horses, still in their harness and still hooked to the wagon. I kept looking but I didn't know what to expect next. I guess I was trying to put it off in some way. Then, there in the wagon under the seat, both of them were hanging on to each other in their last desperate moments. All I could do was cry. It was all over; we fought as hard as we could to get away from that tree but I guess it changed my life forever."

"I'm so sorry, Lorne, I had no idea you had gone through a thing like that. I'm sorry I thought I was the only person in the world that was having to suffer and that I had it worse than anyone else. You've really taught me a good lesson." "Yes mate, I don't believe any of us get away free. I think we all have to suffer our own personal sufferings in some way. Whether we are rich or poor, nobility or commoner, fate can pick on us all."

Edward had to ask Lorne what had happened to his daughter. He told him she was looking after the farm the day they had their wreck. Later on she had gone to be with a young man she married and they had gone to live in Ireland.

It was a beautiful sunny day as they traveled on along the narrow dirt roadway. Edward was beginning to feel comfortable in the presence of this man of strength. They had just shared their experiences of some of the most trying times of their lives. That seemed to relax them and make them feel a little closer to one another. Edward told Lorne he was going to climb in back and take a short nap. "Sure," he said. "There are some wool blankets back there to lie on and cover up with. There is some food down there too."

Edward climbed over the bench they were sitting on and down onto the bed of the wagon and nestled into the blankets there. He felt a little strange at first, having heard the story Lorne had just told him but sleep soon found him. He didn't know how long he had been asleep, when he was suddenly awakened by the sound of a stranger's voice.

He uncovered himself and sat up in the floor of the wagon. As soon as his eyes could focus, he saw soldiers all around the wagon. There were five of them in all. When he came out from under the blanket, the main soldier, doing all the talking said "Oh, I see, you're hiding this child." "No sir," Lorne said. "He is my son!" "My name is Edward," the boy blurted out at the same time Lorne had said, "His name is Henry." The horse soldier quickly spoke up and said, "Now that is interesting; which is it?" Lorne spoke up and said, "His name is Henry Edward Blackard; he is my son." "I see," said the soldier. Then he asked Lorne, "What is your name?" "My name is Lorne Blackard." Then the soldier asked, "Where are you coming from and where are you going to?" "I'm coming from delivering food supplies to Sudeley Castle, near Winchcombe and we are heading back to our farm near Cheltenham." The soldier then asked Lorne, "Who did you deliver the supplies to, in Sudeley Castle?" "I delivered all the goods in the name of Sir Richard, Duke of Gloucester."

"I see," the soldier said. Then the soldier told them, "Carry on and be very careful on your way, there could be lots of fighting going on in this area." "Yes sir," Lorne replied, as he said goodbye to them. The horse soldiers reined their horses around and carried on down the road in back of them.

Lorne and Edward both breathed a deep healthy sigh of relief. "That was close, but please let me do the talking from now on. It's not good for us both to talk at once." "Alright, I will do that," he said to Lorne. As they continued on down the road, Edward was still not fully awake. He started to muse about Lorne calling him his son. *Henry Edward Blackard*, he said over to himself. It actually made him feel kind of warm and proud.

Edward still couldn't forget what Lorne had said to that horse soldier about who that Richard fellow was. So he asked Lorne, "Who was that Richard fellow?" Lorne explained, "He is Edward IV's younger brother, Richard. He is only sixteen but Edward has put him in charge of Sudeley Castle and other castles he has taken possession of around the countryside. Edward is having him trained to take a leadership role in his reign." "So I see, this Richard is holding my mother a prisoner for Edward."

Then young Edward asked Lorne, "Who was that tall soldier that told me not to go upstairs?" Lorne answered, "Oh him, his name is Sir James Tyrrell. He is Richard's personal military trainer. He is well known in the royal circles."[1]

CHAPTER EIGHT

Dream Four: The Homecoming (Part One)

Finally, in their long journey back to Lorne's farm, just outside and north of Cheltenham they came to a good sized meadow. Lorne explained, "This is a good place to stop and water the horses." Edward was more than ready to stop and walk around and relieve himself. He walked down to the river. He wanted to see new country. He loved to fish and he tried to get Lorne to go fishing with him but he had no time for it. After they came back from watering the horses, they laid some blankets out on the sweet smelling meadow grass.

As soon as they got settled Lorne reached into his vest pocket and pulled out a folded piece of paper. He unfolded the paper and showed it to Edward. He could read some, but he didn't want to let Lorne know he could for fear of what this paper might say. The way his life had been going, no telling what it might say, but he was getting schooled pretty fast as to how the world functioned.

"What does that piece of paper have to say that makes you think I should try to read it; what does it have to do with me?" Edward asked Lorne. Lorne then poked the note at him and said, "Can you read at all, lad?" "No!" Edward answered. "Well, I'll read it to you then," Lorne answered.

Lorne started, 'Hello Edward and Lorne. I hope your trip to Sudeley turned out well. We have moved back into the de Wigmore place as we believe it is safe for us to go there now. We have a lot of work to do to fix it up but we are thankful to be back. I shall send five riders to come for Edward on 17 June. Please meet the riders at the Severn

River crossing, one km north of the town of Hereford. Failing that, the riders will come on to the farm. Hope all is well. Can't wait to see you, Edward! Love you both, Kind regards, Jane de Wigmore.'

"Oh no!" Edward complained.

"What's the matter?" Lorne asked.

"I no sooner get back to your place and try to rest for awhile and then I have to leave again on another long horse ride. Then, I have to cross the Severn River again by horseback and ride for another two days back into Wales, then to de Wigmore Cross." The thought of taking that trip was frightening to him. There had been lots of horse soldiers along the roadway when they had gone over to Lorne's farm the first time. They had to ride most of the time in the bush because the roads weren't safe. Edward commented, "Oh well! I may as well grow up and get it over with; at least I am learning new skills that might be of use to me someday."

"Are you quite finished, you little brat?" Lorne spouted quickly and loudly. Then, he grabbed him and rolled him on the ground and started tickling him. They rolled on the ground and it made them both laugh so hard they had tears streaming down their faces. When they finally stopped to catch their breath, they were still lying on the ground in a true resting pose. Then, with a solemn expression, Lorne turned to Edward and said, "Don't forget me, lad. Remember how lucky you were to have had two mothers. Most young people today are lucky to have one. Also remember, it's not how rich we are in money but how much love we have to share."

Edward answered Lorne right away with, "I shall remember you and the things you have taught me. You have helped me through the hardest time of my life so far and I will be thankful to you always." Then Lorne asked, "Do you think you'll like it over at de Wigmore, with Jane and her family?"

"Yes! I have lived with them since I was one month old. How could I think of quitting those people now? They're the only family I have left besides you. Sometimes I've wondered if I would ever see them again."

Lorne then asked, "Where did you live on Snowdon Mountain?"

Young Edward answered, "We lived near a place by the name of Penmynydd. Jane told me that that old castle had been passed down through the old Welsh clans for centuries. Many of the Welsh kings and their wives had their families there. When my mom traded babies with Jane, I was taken back to de Wigmore Castle. Edward IV had been told by one of the kitchen staff about the babies being exchanged. That was when he put my mom under house arrest at Sudeley. Jane got word that Edward was on his way to de Wigmore to find me and have me killed, so I couldn't ever become king. So, that's when we had to leave. We all left and they're back in there now."

Then Lorne said, "Your mom, Jane, told me to look after you until they secured de Wigmore again. She also said she didn't know what kind of condition your mom, Eleanor, was in or if she was still alive. I knew she was alive because of what Margaret Mitchell, the woman you met at Sudeley, told me about her. I go to Sudeley so seldom now since Richard took over there. He got rid of most of his old help and brought in new people. The other servants knew too much and I believe he thought he couldn't trust them anymore. Edward and Richard now control so many castles around the country, they need all the help they can get. Those people have to get new help all the time because they don't want people to know their business." Lorne then said in a solemn voice, "Sorry to change the subject, but we still have a ways to go yet."

"I agree," young Edward replied. With that they both began to prepare the horses and wagon to move. When they got back on the road again they both seemed very calm and relaxed. The stop had done them a wonder of good. The laughing had been like medicine to them both. They seemed to be closer to each other now. They seemed to be getting used to each other's ways. Young Edward started seeing Lorne in a new way. He was a kind person and very knowledgeable. Edward had gained a lot more respect for him now.

Then Lorne asked Edward, "Are you excited to be going to de Wigmore again?" "Yes, I am," Edward responded. "I'll be able to be there with my mom, Jane, again and all the FitzOsberne men. I'll be able to maybe find a girlfriend for my horse Prince, and maybe have some little "Princes" running around in the meadows. I'm so excited about going back there, I probably won't be able to sleep tonight for thinking about it. I have to say though, I'm not excited about crossing the Severn again after hearing about your tragic event."

Lorne said, "Yes, I get all worked up just at the sight of that river, or any river for that matter, anymore. Just remember that when you make your living out on the land, that's the style of life it is and you can't be afraid to live your life. That is just the way it is." Edward then asked Lorne, "Would you go all the way to the crossing where my people are going to meet me." Lorne hesitated, focusing on the horses and the road ahead. Edward didn't want to say anymore for fear of making him feel uncomfortable. Lorne later turned to him and looked into his eyes, and said, "I will do that, lad."

"I'm glad you don't mind doing that, Lorne. I shall be happy for you to meet my mom and all of her people someday," Edward said excitedly. "I shall be happy to meet your mom and all your uncles; how many uncles are there?" Lorne asked. Edward answered with, "There are five of them. Elborne, who brought me to your farm is one of them." "They don't look like horse soldiers or guards to me," Lorne replied. "I know; they don't travel that way. When they are on a mission, they dress as plainly as they can so they don't get killed or robbed," he responded. "How long have you been riding horses?" Lorne asked. "Since I was able to sit up straight in the saddle alone I guess," Edward answered. "Do you like riding horses?" Lorne continued. "Not especially; I'm not keen on riding very long distances. We always have to watch out that soldiers or highwaymen don't attack us. We have to be careful of so many things, it tires me out. That is part of my training for survival I guess, at least that's what they tell me." "Yes, you have had your share of a go at survival, all right." Lorne said laughing.

Then they both laughed a real good hearty laugh. It felt good and they were happy. Edward was looking forward to getting back to the farm even if it was only going to be long enough say hello to the friends he would meet there and then head for his other home again.

Edward then said to Lorne, "Now I get to meet and spend some time with the young boy and girl who work there. Is Louis' name Louis or Lou?" Lorne told him, "His name is Louis Arness, but we just call him Lou. Ellen is Ellen Ann de Lacy but we call her Ellen." "Do you think they will be at the farm when we get back," he asked. Lorne came back with, "I sure hope so; they have to keep the place going when I'm away." They both had a good laugh from Lorne's comment.

Finally, they reached the farm. Edward was glad to be there again even though he had only been there a short time on his last visit. It felt like a home away from home, anyway. They were very tired as they got off the wagon. The horses showed their approval to be home by letting out some big snorts as they came to a standstill. They were tired and hungry too. Ellen and Lou heard the horses come into the farmhouse yard, and came out to meet them and help with everything. They all said their hellos. They hadn't met when Edward was there before because they had been working at other farms in the area. Edward was excited to meet some younger people. This was the first time he was able to meet some new people his own age or at least close to his age.

Lorne then unhooked the horses from their singletrees and they walked them over to the barn. Lorne took off each harness and hung it up on its peg in the cover of the barn. They led the horses to their own stalls and fed them a good meal of oats and hay. They made sure they had water in their buckets outside the stalls.

Then they went back to the wagon and took out what they wanted. They left the rest until morning and pushed the wagon under the cover of the barn. They took off their shoes and went into the house. Ellen had made a big pot of pea soup. It was warming on the wood stove. Edward followed Lorne and went over to the corner and put down their things from the wagon. Then Edward followed Lorne over and washed up at a wooden counter.

They all sat down at the large kitchen table and Lorne said grace. He said, "Thank you, Our Creator, for letting us have a safe trip. Bless all of us here. Look after us, wherever we go. Bless this food to the nourishment of our bodies." They didn't take long eating and not much was said. Ellen and Lou had already eaten and excused themselves early and went on to their beds. They said they would show Edward around the farm in the morning. He told them that would be fun and said his good night to them. He was really looking forward to getting to know them and learning about their way of life. After they finished eating, Lorne showed Edward to his room up-stairs. It was the same room and bed he had used before when he was there. Edward was so tired, he hardly remembered falling asleep.

When he woke again, it was already morning. He put on some clean clothes Ellen had given him of Lou's. He went down stairs and Ellen and Lou were up. Ellen gave him a hot cup of tea. Then, she said, "Boy, from the smell of you, I think you need a bath in the creek and I will wash all your clothes today." "Well, I guess you're right," he tried to defend himself. Then they had a good laugh. Edward then asked how old they were. Ellen said she would soon be nine and Lou said he was eleven. Edward told them he was six but close to seven, to make himself seem older. After all he had just been through, he felt a lot older than that. For breakfast, he ate a bowl of oatmeal and some fresh baked bread Ellen had just made.

After breakfast, they went outside and started a fire so Ellen could teach him to wash his own clothes. He would then have clean clothes to go see his mom and family. By that time, Lorne was up and about and had to go and get the two horses they would ride, and one to pack Edward's belongings on. Edward wanted to tag along with Lorne to see the beautiful meadows and rolling hills. He had a nice cool drink from the creek they got their water from. This setting reminded him of the only home he had known on Snowdon Mountain, in Wales.

They walked down to the meadow and found the horses they needed for the next day's ride. They brought those horses back up to the barn area. Lorne checked the horses' feet and saw they needed to be shod, all three of them, just on their front feet. While Lorne worked on the horses' feet, Edward took his bath in the creek. He was able to get completely naked and dove head first into the creek. The water was so cold he lost his breath, but when he got out of the water and dried off, he felt a lot better. He didn't have any trouble getting to sleep that night.

When he woke up again, it was already morning. Edward got up and put on some of his clean clothes and packed the rest to go on the packhorse and hurried downstairs. Ellen was already up. When he saw her, he said, "You're already up?" "Yes," she answered. Then she added, "I knew you would want to get going early and it is an important day so you want to meet your folks on time." Edward answered, "Yes, you are right, they will want us to meet on time, because it is at least two day's ride from our meeting place to de Wigmore.

It was just Ellen and Edward in the kitchen and she made him some more red clover tea. Then, Ellen said, "Is that your name, Edward de Wigmore?" "Yes," he replied. Lorne then got up and came down to the kitchen. They all said good morning. Lorne again said grace and they ate their porridge in silence.

After breakfast, Lorne was ready to get going. "Will you be ready to leave soon, lad?" Lorne asked. "Yes, I will be," Edward replied. He wanted to say goodbye to Lou, but he was working at the neighbor's farm. "I'll get dressed and go feed and saddle the horses and be ready to leave soon. It will take us about a six-hour steady ride to meet your uncles on time and get you on your way," Lorne said. "I'll get all my clothes and what I'm taking in one bag and bring it out to load," Edward said. Then Lorne got up and went out to do all his chores.

It all happened so fast Edward was saying his final goodbye to Ellen before he knew it. They were shy saying goodbye. He told her he wanted them all to come when these wars were over and spend some time at de Wigmore. He also told Ellen, he would have his own farm someday and he could repay them with the respect they had given him. They had done so much to help him to get through what he had just experienced. He felt more whole now. He felt he had the strength to go on and do what was expected of him in his new home. When he was saying goodbye to Ellen, he embarrassed her by giving her a little kiss on the cheek. He felt like he now had a close friend. He hadn't had that experience before. He had always had guards around him. He never had felt he could be so free.

Lorne brought the horses up to the house and Edward helped load the packhorse. Ellen said her last goodbye to Lorne and him. They both mounted up. It felt surprisingly good to be on horseback again, he thought. He felt really excited about the trip. Lorne and Edward said their final goodbye and just as they were going out of the gate in the front yard, Ellen called out, "Goodbye, my Prince." Edward turned around in his saddle and gave her one last wave. That made him able to laugh whenever he recalled how Ellen called that out to him. The memory would linger with him the rest of his trip home and even beyond that, way beyond.

As they left the farm, the sun was out; it was May and warm. Lorne and Edward hit a good stride and kept it up at a stiff pace. They wanted to make sure they would get across the Severn in the light. When they were getting close to the town of Cheltenham, they started passing men riding in pairs going to small farms in the area. They hadn't encountered any horse soldiers, not yet anyway. They stopped when they were about halfway to where they were supposed to meet Edward's people.

They watered their horses, walked around a little bit and mounted up again and got on their way. They rode on for what seemed a long way and they didn't talk at all; they just rode. Edward was so proud to be riding his horse again. It was gray all over, with black around its eyes. It was so well trained; they were just right for each other. Edward was getting tired of riding but he knew he couldn't think about that.

Later on, Lorne called to him and said, "Let's go on in there." They then stepped up their pace but they could only move as fast as the pack-horse would go. Edward really enjoyed anything to change the pace a bit. Then, he looked up ahead and saw a group of oaks, and then the shining sun's reflection coming off the river. They had reached their destination at the crossing on the Severn River. Edward strained to see if he could see anybody on horseback. They rode on into the camp where they would meet. "No one is here," he said to Lorne. "They'll be here," Lorne spoke up. "We'll cool down the horses and let them have a drink. We can eat and rest. You can get ready for the second half of your trip and I can head back home."

So they finally could dismount and the horses had a good long drink. They took off the horses' bridles and led them to some small willow bushes in the shade and tied them there. They had their bag of food so they had a small picnic. They promptly lay back on the grass and had themselves a good nap. Later on, they didn't know how long it was, there was a tapping on Lorne's right shoulder that ended their nap. When they opened their eyes, they saw a tall man holding the reins of his mount. Looking around, they saw four other men that were close and still mounted on their horses. They both were startled at first but then they realized it was the uncles. Edward gave a shout of delight to see them all again. They had come right up on them without them even knowing it. They'd had lots of practice.

After they had regained their senses, they greeted them all. Edward was so proud to introduce them to Lorne. First there was Elborne, whom Lorne had already met, then there was Jessith, then Wyne, then Sullie, and Owain. These were five brothers of the FitzOsberne clan. Edward then told all of them that Lorne was Lorne Blackard.

In front of the whole group, Owain asked Lorne, "Do you know any of the history of your family name, Blackard?" Lorne answered, "Not all of it, but some." Owain then said, "We are descended from *The Red Branch Knights*. We are also descended from the clan of *The White Boar*." Owain then took off his riding coat and his long sleeved shirt. Then he showed Lorne the insignia of *The White Boar*, sewn on the shoulder of his inside shirt. Owain then explained that they had to ride with that insignia covered up because they had been the guards for the de Wigmore clan. Most of the de Wigmores had been killed off when so many factions were fighting near them in Wales. They couldn't defend themselves any longer so the FitzOsberne clan took them in as part of their clan.

What was now called Mortimer's Cross, on the Wye River a few miles from de Wigmore Castle, was traditionally called de Wigmore Crossing. That was a long time ago. Suddenly, young Edward realized where he had just seen that insignia. He blurted out, "I saw that young soldier and his tall bodyguard wearing them at Sudeley Castle." Owain spoke up, "That bodyguard was James Tyrrell. They have no right whatever to wear our insignia. They have no connection with us at all and know nothing about the history of that mark."

"Well, I've got to go wash up and cool off." As Owain headed down to the river, all the brothers followed. Both Lorne and Edward had just gotten their share of some the old history of the area he would be living in.

Edward now knew the goodbyes to Lorne were at hand. Lorne was sitting on the ground and leaning against a big oak. He got down on his knees and rested his hand on his right shoulder. Lorne then focused on him and Edward began to tell him what he wanted to say. He started by thanking him for being with him and going through a period of his young life that had caused him to grow up very quickly.

Lorne came back with, "Don't let anything that happens to embitter you and don't tell your guts." Edward didn't get a chance to ask him what that meant so he just put it away. He did eventually find out what that statement meant when he asked his mom, Jane, about it. She explained that was an expression used by the elders mostly. She said, "It meant, not to tell too much about yourself or your family or your business in general when talking to people. This saying was to be mostly applied to strangers or people you didn't know so well or who you didn't trust."

Edward was able to use the wisdom of that saying quite often in his life as he got older and was on his own. When in his later life when he had to apply that saying in certain situations, he always was thankful to his mom and Lorne for teaching him that.

Lorne had become like a father to him. It was a new experience and one he wouldn't forget, ever. Lorne gave him a big hug and kissed him on top of his head. He was afraid to look and see if his people were watching. He knew they were. He could tell they liked the way Lorne treated him. They could also tell they got on well and that was good enough for them.

Lorne helped Edward mount and he took the reins. Lorne shook hands with all the clan again. He then asked them to say hello to Jane for him. Edward ask him to please give Lou and Ellen his love. "Farewell, Lorne Blackard," they all said in unison. As they all moved their mounts to the edge of the Severn, Edward then turned and faced Lorne again for a last goodbye and Lorne called to him loudly enough, at least so he could hear, "Goodbye, my prince."

Edward waded into the water to catch up with the rest of the group. The water was calm and shallow. He caught up quickly with the others. As soon as he reached the other shore of the river, he turned his mount and faced the far shore. There was Lorne holding the lines for the other two horses. They gave each other a last wave goodbye. Edward turned onto the trail and started a new adventure which would be part of the fourth and final dream.

CHAPTER NINE
Dream Four: The Homecoming (Part Two)

In the dreams I had, the homecoming turned out to take up a large part of dream four. This dream took in so much detail I had to divide it into three parts. In this part, young Edward's adoptive mother, Jane de Wigmore took him aside one day after he had gone back to de Wigmore Castle for his homecoming. He had already gone to see his real mom, Lady Eleanor.

She began to tell him the true story of what had happened to each of their husbands. In all the time he had spent with Jane, he had never known her not to tell him the truth about things. She told him, "Eleanor's husband, Sir Thomas Boteler and my husband, Owain Rhys-Jones, were on a trip into Wales in February of 1461. They had gone there to try to solicit some Welsh mercenary soldiers to fight against Edward and his army in England.

On their return they had gotten into a battle and both of them were killed. Edward IV's father, Richard of York, had not liked Eleanor's family, the Earls of Shrewsbury, or her married family, the Butler (Boteler) family, because they owned a lot of land and were very powerful politically. Edward IV and his father had made themselves wealthy by killing off certain families who were in opposition to them and their politics, taking their land and wealth.

Jane told young Edward what had happened with him up until then. She thought he was now mature enough to know about questions he had of his young past.

She began, "Your mother's Sudeley Castle was taken over by King Edward. Her husband died in battle in the War of the Roses. So then your mother had gone to see if she could get Sudeley Castle back from Edward. Now the story becomes muddled.

"Your mother then supposedly married Edward. He then had intercourse with her. From that contact your mom became pregnant and that is how you came to be born. If the precontract marriage, as it was known then, was carried out, which I know it was, your father didn't want anyone to know this for, as his legitimate son, in the future your mother could have been able to claim the crown of England in your name. That is why Eleanor knew she had to find a new home for you. She believed Edward would have you killed. Edward didn't want to have your mother killed because it wouldn't look good for him when he had just become the new King of England.[1]

"Your mom Eleanor, became pregnant with you in late March of 1461 and you were born 12 December that same year. When she knew she was going to have you, Edward was away fighting his battles and wasn't there when you were born. When I had my son, he died of the fever at birth. Your mom found out about my son dying from a horse messenger I had sent and she sent a message back to me by the same horseman. In the message I received, she told me to bring my deceased son to Sudeley Castle, then we would exchange babies. So, I wrapped my son in a nice blanket and said my goodbyes to him. The next morning the horse messenger took him to your mom at Sudeley. When your mom received my son's body, she quickly hid his body so it could be buried as soon as she could arrange it. Again in secrecy, she wrapped you in a warm wool blanket. Then she had her man servant give you to the horse messenger as secretly as could be done and hoped no one had noticed."

Young Edward then interrupted Jane, to ask her what her son's name was. She answered him with, "His name was Larson, after his uncle and his great-grandfather." Young Edward said, "I will always remember his name."

Jane continued, "We both had decided to exchange our babies because we thought if Eleanor could tell Edward that her child had died in childbirth, Edward would not feel threatened by this newborn son that supposedly had not lived. That is why everyone thought you had died at birth or shortly after.

"Please know that both Eleanor and I cried for days but we both knew it might be the only way that you could live and be protected by my people. Your mom took great joy in that and knew full well she was taking a risk but she felt she had to take that chance. Secretly, she wanted you to become a king someday. She loved you so very much and I still do."

He started crying and Jane reached out and held him. They grew to love each other very much.

Young Edward had already been told most of what was being told to him by his adoptive mother, Jane, by his birth mother, Lady Eleanor. He was very happy to hear the story from Jane as well because when he had been with Eleanor, time was of the essence and he didn't have time to ask many questions.

Jane went on to say, "We had the horse messenger bring you by horseback over into Wales to de Wigmore Castle, where we were waiting to receive you. We both thought everything was fine until Edward returned to Sudeley Castle and one of the house servants told him what had transpired in his absence, concerning the exchange of two new-born babies.[2]

"Edward IV talked to Lady Eleanor about what he had been told. She told him that their son had died at birth and she had to have the manservant bury the child in the west-tower garden. The King became extremely angry with both Eleanor and me and the whole FitzOsberne clan, when he learned we had tricked him. This is why Lady Eleanor was then put into chains in the upper tower chamber of Sudeley Castle. That is where she would remain until she finally starved to death. She was buried in that west-tower garden, as well as my child. That would have been the only garden she would have been able to view for the many days before her life was finished." [3]

In reprisal, Edward IV took his army in and drove them all out and took over de Wigmore Castle.[4] Some of Edward's army were Welsh mercenaries who didn't like the de Wigmore clan. The reason for that was that they had been one of the ruling clans in that area. They had been friends with the old FitzOsberne clan because they had both migrated to England from Normandy after the invasion in 1066. They had originally built de Wigmore Castle out of logs. For many years both families had, in times past, been very well off. Edward IV had taken de Wigmore Castle to use to his advantage because he could stable enough horses and men inside of it; he had fought some of his most decisive battles from there.

From information I had gathered mostly from my dreams about de Wigmore Castle, I learned it was built on what was called a hog's back ridge, with two levels of stables. From my dreams I knew that there was enough room to stable at least fifty horses and troops, full combat ready, on each level. The bottom level contained a tunnel, made out of stone, which opened out onto a back wooded area with enough hills to cover the troops without much exposure. The upper level stables were able to house fifty more combat-ready horses and opened into another wooded area downhill, in front of the castle. I could well see why Edward wanted to use that castle to fight his battles from in that area. It was well built and at a good crossroads position.

Edward's Yorkist troops had fought and defeated the Lancastrian troops from de Wigmore Castle in 1461. That had given Edward enough victory to go to London to claim his right as king; it paid off for him and he was well received.

After Edward had won the victories he was after by using de Wigmore Castle, he purposely had his army destroy as much of the castle as they could. He did this because he had been tricked and he did not like the de Wigmore's hiding his son, young Edward de Wigmore.

In dream four, Jane and her people where able to go back there and fix up enough of the castle for her family clan to live in there again. Young Edward de Wigmore was happy to know he was going to be able to go back there to live.

From all the research I have done on Edward IV's reign, the feeling I get is he had singled out those families because they were Irish, they had wealth, they had political power, lots of land and they were Catholic and Lancastrains. They were Lady Eleanor's family and her husband's family. Edward crushed the whole lot of them and took their wealth and Lady Eleanor's, as well.

CHAPTER TEN

Dream Four: The Homecoming (Part Three)

A t first, I seemed at a loss to explain this part of the story. I believe that was because this chapter was such an isolated segment which came to me later than the other three dreams. Also, it was in the order of the other dreams being the latter part of dream three. What troubled me here so much is I didn't have this dream until I had recorded my notes on all three of the other dreams. This dream four seemed to be a review of the three other dreams. I had learned some information about dreaming in the research I had already done. In some ways I felt I had more of an advantage in experiencing this dream than all the rest I had worked on so far.

I felt more confident going into this dream because I didn't seem to have so many of my older feelings of doubt about what was happening. I knew more about what to expect. Again though, I felt after the dream was over and being a critical person, that I had designed this dream to fit a sort of "they lived happily ever after" pattern. Then I realized I was fortunate to have written down as much of this whole story as I did, considering what an unusual type of communication this was.

In the overall I found with this dream four a tenet that seemed to have been held in common in all four dreams. There was a type of non-linear expression that seemed to contain what I call a "symbolic code," of some kind. This code seemed to be exemplified in the form of little hints or clues to make me want to follow these clues to see where that would lead. That way, one dream became built into another until they all joined together.[1]

All of the information that was coming through the dreams was not always given in an orderly pattern. I had to take the information given and fill in the blank places and see in what direction it would go. Then I was able to compare the dream information to the written history.

A perfect example of this occurred when I was studying the historical information about Edward IV's stronghold of de Wigmore Castle where he won his first and significant victory. That statement led me to lock in on the name de Wigmore Castle. That is how I found out when I studied Edward's life, what that family name and that castle had to do with my past life. In the end of the story it was a known fact that Lady Eleanor and Edward IV did have a son. Supposedly, Edward named him Edward de Wigmore.[2]

I had often wondered who named young Edward. I noticed they didn't label him a Plantagenet as his father was. I don't think it would have been his father that named him but I guess the historians, at least most of them, thought he died at birth anyway, so it didn't really matter what his name was.

According to Thomas Costain, in his book *The Three Edwards*, Edward II had taken de Wigmore Castle in his reign. Then it was taken over by Edward II's wife, Queen Isabella, and her consort Roger de Mortimer who then became the 8th Baron of Wigmore. Therefore, I believe Edward IV thought that it was his birthright to take over de Wigmore Castle.

Finally, I was able to go back to my original notes from dream one. The answer I finally came up with was that young Edward's mother in the dreams birthed him as the son of Edward IV. Then she had him sent to Jane de Wigmore, her friend, when he was a baby, to be raised by her. He was told by Eleanor that Jane never legally adopted him but that's the agreement they made with each other. Edward found out his son had been sent by Eleanor to de Wigmore Castle in order to save his life. Still in dream one, Edward did, I believe, go looking for him to have him killed, so he would not be able to claim the throne as the son of a king in the future. I also remember from the dreams that Edward de Wigmore lived a long and prosperous life to the age of about 76.[3]

When Edward IV arrived at de Wigmore Castle, Jane de Wigmore, her guardians and young Edward were nowhere to be found. So, he felt betrayed by Eleanor and Jane. In his anger, he had his men destroy part of the castle. But as I was to learn later, Edward destroyed some of that castle to keep his opposing forces from using it to go on fighting him.

Edward was used to getting his way but young Edward's new family had eluded him. At first, dream four seemed almost to be another book in itself. I couldn't stop writing my notes out by hand long enough to be able to organize anything to incorporate into the story. It was very difficult to remember what had transpired in this dream. I had come in contact with the de Wigmore name and the woman named Jane who in the dreams was called Jane de Wigmore.

She had explained in the dream that de Wigmore was her real family name, but when so much of her family had been killed off, the FitzOsbernes had taken the remaining members of her family under their protection in the early part the 11th century. William FitzOsberne had always designed and built castles and he was responsible for building de Wigmore Castle. They had built both of the castles she was now in charge of. The area of de Wigmore was an ancient Celtic settlement and she said her ancestors had taken on the FitzOsberne name for their own protection. The village today is called Wigmore.

I found in further research that William FitzOsberne was a distant cousin of William the Conqueror but that is hard to prove. William FitzOsberne worked with building castles in England and Wales, with a man named Odo, The Bishop of Bayeux. He was a half brother of William the Conqueror.

I was anxious to find out what, if anything, still remained of de Wigmore Castle. I found that what was left of it stands in the northwest corner of Herefordshire a few kilometers from the current boundary between England and Wales. I had learned in my research from various tour companies, this once was one of the largest castles in that area and it was built by Earl William FitzOsberne, who had become the Earl of Hereford in 1066. He was supposed to have died in the battle of Cassel in Flanders in 1071. After Earl William's death, his son, Roger of Breteiul was imprisoned for life in 1075 after a failed rebellion against William the Conqueror. That seems odd that Roger would have brought a rebellion against William the Conqueror, because both his father, Earl William and himself were related to him and always built castles for him.

William I was employing Earl William and his son to build lots of castles around Wales and England. I have already located four castles that Earl William had built. In 1078 Earl William built Carisbrook Castle and in 1087, William the Conqueror ordered Earl William FitzOsberne to build Norwich Castle. I found that strange because he was supposed to have died on the battlefield in Flanders in 1071. The main question I had about Earl William going to fight in Flanders was why would William I have risked one of his best castle builders to go fight in a war and get killed. That didn't make any sense. Those dates have a gap of 7 and 16 years between the time Earl William would have died at Flanders. All the history I have read about Earl William had stated he died in 1071. I know that dates in history that far back can be wrong at times. I am curious about those dates being wrong twice in a row.[4] I believe he and his son Roger of Breteiul were murdered because they were getting too politically powerful with the help of a man named Odo, the Bishop of Bayeux.

Today I understand the massive site of de Wigmore Castle is covered in ruins and ditches of a fortress. In my dreams of de Wigmore Castle, the outer keep contained the original remains. The bottom chamber, which could house 50 troops and horses, as I have previously mentioned, is now covered under many centuries of plant growth. As I have already explained, the bottom chamber had a covered exit by way of a rock-walled tunnel. This tunnel had been dug into the back or eastern exit, to give cover to the troops as they emerged out into what was then a nearby forest. The western tunnel exit allowed troops to emerge far enough down the hillside to allow good cover. I drew my drawing of how I perceived de Wigmore Castle only from my dreams of it.[5]

I still don't know how the structure and linear progression of the four dreams came into their evolving order. My question to myself was, *How could such a conscious event present itself in a perfect material order?* Then I had to remind myself I had spent hours and days to put it in that order! I am still working on putting the dreams into an understandable order. The only answer I could come up with was we see everything in our life the way we were taught or we have learned to see them as children and that's how we will see our life's events for its duration.

I mentioned in the beginning of this manuscript, when the first dream occurred, it was all I could do to try to follow the story line. I don't like linear thinking but I believe that is how we organize our dreams. Even then, we do have dreams that don't seem to follow much of a pattern at all. I believe our minds must somehow take in the energy of dreams in a non-linear structure. Then the dream is deciphered and translated into a type of linear order that we can understand. I believe our dreams are then run through a brain computer system and put into the language we are accustomed to using.

I believe that we dream in the languages we speak, but I don't know what happens when we are multi-lingual. I have always dreamed in English. All of the dreams I had for this project were in English and that seemed normal. As for Edward's mothers in these dreams, Eleanor was Anglo-Irish; Jane was Welsh. Luckily in the dreams, they both spoke English. Now, I carry on with the story of this dream four.

As young Edward de Wigmore, or Henry Edward Blackard, whatever the occasion called for, was moving back to his beloved adoptive mother, Jane de Wigmore, he mused about what was becoming his home place again. He could only imagine it in his dreams. He was too young, just a baby, when he had first been taken there. Then they all had to leave and go into Mount Snowdon.

He learned to love that place in the mountains. It was old and had been in Jane's family for centuries. It was first constructed of heavy wooden beams. That became the whole inside structure. The stone, of almost magical quality, was added many years later. He got to experience the wood and the stone construction together. As a side note, I still have not found the name of that castle in Mount Snowdon.

Young Edward would always remember with fondness the snow-capped Mount Snowdon, the cold mountain springs, his secret fishing holes and his favorite horses. He had all a young lad his age could ever hope for. He remembered hoping that the old castle would remain the same as he remembered it when he had to leave it. He was still thrilled by the idea of going back there. It was like starting a whole new life. He longed to go back and pay Mount Snowdon a visit someday.

As they traveled on, he always stayed as close as he felt comfortable riding among these men. They were the guards of de Wigmore, who had come to get him and escort him home. He felt very important to be cared for like that. When they cleared the area of the town of Cheltenham, they changed their direction more to the northwest. They were going now on a trail he had never seen and they were heading for a place known in the area as Mortimer's Cross. The de Wigmore Castle was about five more kilometers west on the trail past Mortimer's Cross as he understood. He wanted to ask the guards what it looked like but they were very quiet and only talked among themselves and not much of that. They had to go through the country very quietly and move quickly.

The FitzOsberne clan, as young Edward came to know them, were a very military family. They told him once that they belonged to an ancient order named the "Order of the Golden Fleece," founded in the 11th century. He couldn't understand all of what they told him about that, but he listened to them and looked at them when they spoke to him. That was part of the manners he had been taught. All he knew was they had been responsible for them all getting out of de Wigmore and getting through the mountains in the dead of winter. They had taken him to be with Lorne Blackard, so he could meet his birth mother, Lady Eleanor, for the first and last time before she passed away. Now, they were taking him back home again. When he thought about how they had looked after his new mother Jane and him, he really did start to feel like a real prince. He wasn't sure what that felt like but it was good to know he had people looking after him and teaching him new things and most of all, giving him a family to be a part of.

What caught his attention was the fact that these guards were military men but they dressed so plainly when they came to meet him and take him back home to de Wigmore. They wore what was called peasant dress, which was plain colors or only two colors of clothes. He found this very odd because they wore the clan colors at home, in Snowdon. They wore their dark green and black plaids. Soon he realized as he watched them riding ahead of him, that even the tack they were using on their horses had been changed over to all their old torn-up saddles and bridles. No good clean tack was used on the horses when they were traveling like this. He finally realized they were doing this to not be recognized as a military group because they were passing through a live war zone at that time.

Finally, as they rode out into an open area from the forest they had just passed through, they reined in their horses and came to a stop. Edward wondered what was going on now. He suddenly started watching the woods that they had all just come from, to see if there was anyone following them. They all laughed at him at first but then they consoled him by saying, "That was a good habit to develop, to always watch your rear." Then he calmed down when they said, "We only stopped to re-group and talk about what we will do for the rest of our ride back to de Wigmore."

Young Edward was assigned to ride with Wyne and Sullie. He was to ride in the middle with Wyne ahead and Sullie in back of him. Aber, Jessith and Owain would ride ahead of them to look like they were a separate group. They would, however, keep them in sight at all times. They were both to signal each other if anything was coming their way. So after they had watered their horses, they remounted and took their various positions in their planned formation.

When they had ridden for most of the day, they found a place to stop. They regrouped and dismounted to give the horses a break and watered them after they cooled down a little. Edward was beginning to need some food. One thing for sure was these men weren't big on eating while they were on the move. In these times of war all around them, they wanted to get from one place to the next as quickly as possible and not be noticed. After Edward had watered his horse, he sat down under a nice shade tree and opened his small bag of food.

They had gone off the main trail at a place by a stream. They were careful to travel on a rock patch until they were well off the main trail. They didn't want anyone to see their tracks or see them all together. They were always careful of that. They were well hidden in a grove of trees. These men knew all the safe spots to stop at because they had used these trails for many years, just as their ancestors had. This was an important part of their survival.

Soon after they had stopped for a rest and the horses were watered and tied, Wyne came over and sat down beside Edward. Wyne asked how he was holding up and Edward told him he was getting tired and hungry. He also told him he was sure excited to be going to see de Wigmore and especially, his mom. Wyne then explained to him, with caution not to frighten him too much, what was about to take place.

Wyne began by saying they would pass by Ludlow Castle. Edward IV and his Yorkest army had been using as many Welsh border castles as they could. Wyne also went on to explain how Ludlow was built on an area that used to belong to a Marcher lord named Josse de Dinant, in the reign of Henry I. Dinant had fought a perpetual struggle to hold Ludlow against both the Welsh and two powerful fellow nobles, Hugh Mortimer and Walter de Lacy. That brief history lesson was a thing they would usually do with him as they traveled through different areas of the country. Wyne thought it was good for Edward to know about areas he might be traveling in again sometime.

Wyne went on to tell young Edward that they didn't know what to expect when they were going by Ludlow Castle. They didn't know if there would be troops stationed there or not. Wyne said they thought Edward IV would be in France, trying to round up more troops to continue his present war against Henry VI. He also told him that this war was referred to as the "War of the Roses." Young Edward said without thinking, as he often did, "That's an odd name for a war." Wyne didn't show any response to his wise remark but instead told him that Edward's army were known as the Yorks. Their symbol was the white rose. Henry's army were known as the Lancasters, who used the red rose as their symbol. He thanked Wyne for explaining this to him. He had heard them talking among themselves at different times but he really didn't know who was who, but he was glad he knew now.

In their conversation with each other, Wyne made sure to warn him to remain calm if they met any troops on the way. Once they were past Ludlow Castle, they would then move more to the west up by Mortimer's Cross. They would then move up to cross the Severn River and from there they would head for home. He also added they would be traveling most of the last leg of the trip in the dark. Edward hardly heard the part about traveling in the dark, because he was so focused on the words, "Head for home." He got a thrill in the pit of his stomach every time he repeated those words to himself. He was truly thankful he still even had a home to head for.

At that point he didn't care what he had to go through to get there. It seemed as though he had moved around all over the place since he was born. Now he felt he would just love to be with his mom and feel happy and safe. He was sick of wars and didn't want to travel through war areas any more. He never said anything to any of the men about how he felt about war. Even in his young mind, he had already seen how war had made him so cautious when he had to travel anywhere. He had always been afraid, since he knew what fear was. He had already had lots of practice in just being able to stay as far away from it as he could, just to try to survive. Even his adopted family had to move and live in other places until it was safe enough to go back. Still, he harbored a secret thought he had never shared with anyone. That was an ever present thought of *What if Edward comes back again sometime to take me; then what will I do?* He carried that thought with him on into his later life until he knew for sure both Edward and his brother, Richard, were dead and he didn't have to fear them any longer. He knew though, that Henry was now king and he knew he would have him killed if he ever found him.

Wyne had also told him a story about a man named Hugh de Montgomery who had ravaged the Isle of Anglesey. In that time, the crossing they were going to cross was known as Montgomery Crossing. Then Wyne laughed and said, "The crossing should have been called de Wigmore Crossing because the whole area we are going to cross into was in very old times called de Wigmore by the old Anglo-Saxons. This was long before these new people came," he explained. Edward felt a certain pride in what Wyne had told him about the history of the area he was going to have as his new home.

As they mounted up again, Wyne told them to make sure they all had their daggers in their sheathes, inside the top of their boots. When they had started this journey, Wyne had given young Edward his dagger in a leather sheath and had shown him how to keep it hidden inside his boot. He hoped he would never have to use it, but it was there all the same. Edward never knew what might happen in these times. He took a kind of odd comfort looking down into his right boot top and seeing the dagger there.

The horses knew their way back onto the main trail. These men had to be careful and follow their same way back onto the trail. As they took their places in the formation, Edward began to relax. He started thinking about what was happening to him in his life at this time. He thought, in the overall, he was pretty introspective for a young lad. He had to realize he hadn't been with any people his own age yet. At the same time he realized here he was, traveling along a well traveled roadway, with these military men who were his personal bodyguards, who had taken him in and saved his life. Now they were continuing to protect him and trying to provide him with a family and a home, the same as Lorne Blackard had done for him. This let him know there were still good people in his war-torn world.

As they rode, he began to see, off in a distant clearing, a large castle. He turned in his saddle and fell back to ask Wyne if the castle he was seeing was Ludlow and Wyne confirmed it was. He felt at that moment that he was seeing the history of his life passing before him. He marveled at the seeming strength of that massive structure, even at a distance. Suddenly, at the top of a big knoll, they saw Aber flash a sign. That sent a fright through Edward's whole body! Wyne and Sullie then flashed a hand signal back to let them know they got the message. They all then sat up straight and tall in their saddles. Wyne pulled up right beside him on his left and Sullie came up close on the right of him. Wyne could see how frightened he was and he told him, in a low voice, just to stay calm and pretend they were farmers, going to buy some milk cows at Shrewsbury. Wyne said, "That is our story; think about nothing else." He also told him to use his Blackard name if they asked him. Edward's mind was a total blank. He had a great urge to turn his horse around and head off into the bush. He held on and he could see and feel the total strength of these two men and it helped settle him. He suddenly remembered going through this same exercise with Lorne and that helped him get ready to cope with this encounter.

Then they all saw four horseman, in military dress, come into view. They were riding four-abreast and were taking up most of the road. Wyne and his men, moved over to the side of the road to yield to them, just as was expected of them. As they came ever closer to them, the oncoming soldiers fixed them in their stare. When the soldiers got right up to them, close enough to make eye contact, they stopped in front of them.

Wyne greeted them and they started asking him the questions. First they asked if they were with those other three men they had seen up ahead on the road. Wyne told them no and that they didn't know the other men were there. Wyne's group all waited for a big response to that answer. Edward quickly had a thought run through his mind. He thought, true military men would have known someone was ahead on the trail because of their fresh tracks or fresh horse manure. Then to his surprise, they asked the same question Wyne had told him they might ask.

They asked him where they were going. Wyne answered that they were heading for the town of Shrewsbury, to purchase some milk cows. Edward felt a heavy pause, as the soldier asking all the questions suddenly looked directly at all three of them, as though he was trying to read all of their faces and minds at once. All the men Edward was with knew the body language of military officers. They all seemed to hold their breath as they waited for the next move in this "mental chess game." Evidently, the officer asking all the questions, finally got the reaction on their faces that he was satisfied with and finally said, "OK, carry on."

With that, all three of them wished them good-day and when they were out of view, Wyne and his men carried on down the trail. Finally, Edward felt he could breathe and swallow again. As they settled into their pace once again, he wondered how the other men had faired. They hadn't contacted them, so they thought everything was still in order. As they rode on, everyone seemed to be alone with his own thoughts, mulling over what had just taken place. Perhaps trying to score their performance as to how well they had answered the questions. That's what Edward was doing anyway. Wyne broke the silence with, "I sure am glad that officer didn't ask me where our farm was." Sullie quickly asked, "What would you have said if he had?" Then they all laughed quietly and Wyne said, "We would have been in deep trouble." Wyne also said to Edward later, "They like to ask the younger riders questions because they aren't as good at knowing how to answer as the older men are."

Edward remembered being asked questions by the military men Lorne and he had run into when they were traveling together. He remembered he had almost gotten in trouble there. The men had always taught him to be very aware of every move he made and every word he said, whether it be in a war zone or not, because one slip-up could cost him and others their lives.

As they rode on and got in the rhythm of their movement along the trail, Edward felt himself begin to relax a little more. Later on he began to think about this new family he was already a part of. When he saw a chance, he asked Wyne, because he had such a good memory of the family history where his family had come from.

Wyne explained their family had come originally from Denmark, from a place named Alborg. They were people who worked with wood and built houses and boats. They went into the area of France called Normandy. When they settled in France they married into the FitzOsberne family. After they were there for a few years they traded a house they had built for a beautiful sailboat. The sailboat was named *de Etoile Filante*, or "The Shooting Star." They sailed to Cardiff, Wales first and settled there for a few years. Then they were sent to the area they were in now. When they got to build their first castle in Wales they called the area de Wigmore, as well as the castle. They were stonecutters too, and could build with stone as well as wood. A lot of the old castles were first built out of wood and later replaced with stone.

When Edward was about 15 years old, his mother Jane was able to get Lorne and Ellen to come to de Wigmore. Edward had grown to be a tall and happy teen and was very mature for his age. Jane was getting on in years and wanted to do something very special for him while he was still a young man. She secretly arranged to have Lorne and his housekeeper come to de Wigmore. She had wanted to do something special for them because they had treated young Edward so well when he had stayed with them nine years ago.

They would be there soon. Jane couldn't stop thinking about it. She felt good that the war was finally over, for the most part, and now was a good time to travel the country again and not worry too much about getting robbed and or killed. Lorne and Ellen did arrive there. They were very tired, but the FitzOsberne clan welcomed them and treated them as truly special guests. Edward was totally surprised and extremely happy.

The company loved finally coming to de Wigmore Castle, what was left of it when Edward IV had gotten finished with it. That was alright with Lorne and Ellen. They were just very happy to come and meet everyone there. They felt at ease to see young Edward at home in his beautiful surroundings. They were especially happy to meet Jane for the first time and as well to meet the FitzOsberne clan.

So the story went, and it was quite a story in the country round about. Eventually, Jane arranged to marry Lorne and they adored each other and were very content with the bond they had made. The biggest shock Edward had with this part of the story was he ended up marrying Ellen some years later. Soon after they had gotten married, he took Ellen over to Anglesey Island in northern Wales.

On the way there, he told Ellen a story Owain had told him, of when they had gone there for the first time together after young Edward had just returned back to de Wigmore. Owain said when they arrived in Anglesey he had been standing, gazing at some massive stones, stacked up together in a field. Then Owain said he heard a branch crack and turned around to see an elderly man who came out of the wooded area and right up to him. Owain said hello to him and instead of returning any greeting, the man looked at him, to make sure he had his attention. Then the man said, "Sometimes our dreams can be deceiving, and sometimes we sacrifice ourselves to our dreams." With that, the man turned and went back into the woods in the direction he had come from. Owain said, for awhile he didn't know if that encounter had happened or not! He said it was so strange, he never forgot it.

That had always been one of young Edward's favorite places, when the FitzOsbernes had taken him there he had seen the Druid cromlechs, for the first time. Now, when they arrived there, they had walked into a wooded area and there, Ellen saw these large stones on smaller upright pillars. She had never seen anything like that before and she immediately turned to Edward and asked, "How could they have gotten those large stones up onto those small stone pillars like that?"

Edward quickly responded, "Oh, that's nothing, they just dug down under those big stones until they could get the pillars in under them and standing up. Then they dug the rest of the dirt out from under the big stone and that was it." Then, Ellen said, "Really!" Edward then came back with, "I don't know, I just thought it was a good possibility." Then Ellen told him, looking him right in the eyes, "You are such a dreamer!"

They too were very content with the whole way of life they would live now. This de Wigmore Castle had not seen this much activity and happiness for many years. The FitzOsbernes had said many times that it just wasn't the same old place—it was a lot better! To see horses and cows and sheep and children running everywhere around this old castle, brought tears to the eyes of the "old soldiers." They had all worked very hard to have it that way. It had truly been worth the struggles they had all found themselves in. They were there to enjoy it now with all who came there.

Edward took both of them, Ellen and Lorne and showed them his very favorite spots and the beautiful rolling hills and tall grasses. So the story went and it was quite a story in the country around there. Jane arranged to marry Lorne and they each invited special guests. Edward remembered he was totally surprised and extremely happy with all that was happening with his life now. He truly felt as though he really had a wonderful family around him. They were people whom he loved and they had all tried hard to make it that way.

CHAPTER ELEVEN
The Mental Realm Of The Dreams

I have always had problems remembering peoples' names. When I had the dreams relating to this story, I was so taken by the oddity of what was taking place that I didn't remember hearing Lady Eleanor's last name. I don't recall it ever being mentioned. I remembered Jane de Wigmore's and young Edward de Wigmore's whole names. I began slowly searching for both of them in the history books I started using as my references. When I first encountered both of them in the dreams, I was so mystified by all the happenings that were taking place seemingly at once.

Little did I know how many Eleanors there would be that I would have to research closely to find the one these dreams were focused on. I was so preoccupied by the novelty of that phenomenon. I realize that getting caught up in that feeling cost me a lot of unnecessary searching to find the Eleanor I was looking for. It almost seemed I was being made to search for her so I would find a lot out about her background to build this story from.

The key here was that when the woman was talking to young Edward, she had told him he was her son by Edward IV. I had forgotten that detail because I was still in shock from having had the dream. If I would have gone straight to the research on Edward IV, I would have found the Eleanor I was looking for right away. As a consolation I still got a good background understanding of the history of that time period that I may not have gotten otherwise. I needed all the information I could get. It would have been very difficult and maybe impossible to write this book without very extensive research anyway. I learned about shortcuts that can be taken in writing any kind of history. Later on, I would learn to use what I refer to as "keys and fragments"[1] to help me build the research needed for this kind of undertaking.

I had realized from the Coat of Arms I had purchased that both sides of my families had been living and had contacts in Denmark, Normandy, Orkney Islands, England, Ireland and Wales. They had lived in England at least since about 1066 A.D. and in the same geographic locations in which this story takes place. I had no idea that both sides of my ancestral families went that far back. I realized these dreams had already helped me to find personal information I may never have known about. Now I felt more equal to the task after researching information that happened over 900 years ago.

As I have mentioned already, an interesting idea came to me in the beginning of trying to formulate how this manuscript should be written. I began to wonder if I may have provoked or programmed these dreams into becoming a reality in my present life. But when the dreams started occurring, I didn't know anything about this part of English history and nothing about my own families' histories. I got myself off of that hook by reasoning that I couldn't use my mind to program something I had no idea of. I just wanted to work on what I knew for sure had happened in my dream experience but it seemed at first I wasn't sure of anything.

Now at this point, I could be a real braggart and start waving the flag and say, if you really want to know about your past, just go for it. Then a caution flag went up. On the other side of this issue, I want to lend a little advice to the reader by saying that finding out who you are and where you came from is perhaps not for everyone. We are dealing with an extremely delicate and gray area of our mental thresholds here. I'm not posing as a mental therapist or doctor. I have no training in these disciplines at all. In writing a book such as this, I had to tell myself there are people who are not willing to know what went on in their past life or lives and they may not care to find out.

When I first started thinking about sharing this experience with anyone else other than my wife, it seemed I was feeling a lot of doubt or guilt about even having had these dreams. In the beginning, I was trying to make excuses for them. For me now, as I look back, I realize it has been a few years, since 1994, between having these dreams and even beginning to bring myself to try to make them into a readable story. Finally, with all the false starts I seemed to have had, now I have written these dreams down and I am working with the material I have gathered over the years. I am finally weaving this story together. It's still a long process to sort out all the information I want to use. Then, I had to sort out the conflicting material from that period of history. A very positive factor here is that the memory of these dreams is as sharp today as when each of them came to me because I have had to go back over them so many times to piece them together.

I realize now, since I have had the experience of these dreams, I am spurred on by wanting to seriously learn all I can about my past life or lives and what I may have experienced in them. I believe now there is such a thing as past lifetimes. Also, I thought if I could understand what happened in my past life or lives, I may be able to understand my present life better. I also entertain the thought of this experience helping me become a better person. In the process of developing the story to build a publication around, I realized I had only the bare minimum of a glimpse into only one yester world, encapsulated in these four minuscule dreams.

Young Edward had only a very few precious moments to see and hear this woman in the upstairs tower of Sudeley Castle in the first dream. Visually, the figure was tall and slender. She was fine boned, with a sharp thin nose and high, delicate cheekbones. Her hair was long but matted and it was as black as coal. When she spoke to him, he was amazed at how soft spoken she was but also, how well he could hear her and understand everything she was saying to him.[2]

Her voice had such a kind demeanor and her speech was well composed. He found that notable because of the stressful conditions she was living under. Upon first meeting her, young Edward could hardly understand how she could still speak at all. Even at his young age, in his only encounter with her, he realized her mind seemed still fully intact and clear. He could see purpose and intent in her eyes. She didn't seem to let the conditions she was existing in interfere with what her true focus was there. Young Edward had no idea what that focus was.

Finally, when she did speak to young Edward, she explained, "I am your mom, my name is Eleanor and I am the Queen of England. Your name is Edward de Wigmore and you are a prince. You are my prince and my only son." From that one detail and many hours of research, I was finally able to determine that this person was Lady Eleanor Talbot-Butler. That in itself was a long process of elimination of the many different women named Eleanor, in this long period of history.

My research covered a period of English history from about the 1150s, when Henry II took Eleanor of Aquitaine as his wife, and ended with Edward IV marrying Lady Eleanor Talbot-Butler in early March 1461. I discovered a feeling of self-criticism, which I had when I first started contemplating writing this book. At first, as I have mentioned before, I thought "No, you're just making this all up. So what, you had a dream. It could have been something from a movie you saw once. It could have been pure fantasy."

I knew deep inside though, that I hadn't made this story up. I couldn't stand the history of the Middle Ages anyway. I thought, *Why would I go and make up some story about something I know nothing of and care even less about?* That is the crux of the reason I stuck with this story. If we need a reason to do or not to do things, then my guess is the story chose me, I didn't choose it.

It took me a long time after having had these dreams, to actually begin doing anything concerning them. The serious research I would have to complete on all that history that I never wanted to look at was mind boggling. I am still working on the research. Sometimes I find myself wondering if I will ever finish; it seems to be endless. I had to realize history doesn't stop; it is always happening around us. I guess what took so long in even deciding to begin doing any serious active research was being caught up in my own personal life in general. The most inhibiting factor I believe was being afraid of what family and friends would say. I could just hear them, *Boy, he's really gone off the deep end this time.*

Finally, I had to decide to work on this manuscript or just totally forget it. I knew it wasn't a part-time choice. So, as you can see I made my choice to start doing the research and go on with it and see where that would take me. I had never written a book as such. The experience of writing all this as a volume was totally foreign to me. This was an arduous affair and time consuming at that. I just had to justify the time spent, and my efforts on all this research, as a kind of hobby because I surely wasn't making any money at it.

Many people can't spend time working at something on a non-monetary basis, even though they still find it fun and interesting. Like most people, I have had to work to stay alive. A person has to work at something that brings in some monetary benefits, or they run a risk, as so many people do with a type of artistic bent. The risk is of being labeled, non-productive, lazy or just plain dreamers!

At first, I didn't tell anyone that I was working on research for a book. I still wasn't really sure I was up to the task of trying to put all this information into a logical and readable form. It wasn't as easy as I had thought it would be. The urge to actually put it all on paper came in short runs. At times, I put it away for months. At other times, when I would start up again, I couldn't stop. My father always used to say I was a dreamer. Well, I'm proud of it now. Maybe the world needs more dreamers.

Even though these dreams I'm researching have had such an impact on me, I still have to spend a lot of time developing the minute details of the dreams, in order to make them understandable, even to me. When I started this project as I have said before, I was not in the least up on the War of the Roses period of history. I had never taken any courses on that period of history in university. I had to study the five Eleanors. I had found some women that were prominent during most of the historical time frame I had isolated to study. I wanted to study these five and see if their history would fit into the mold or pattern of characteristics I had experienced in the dreams.

Also, my own primitive intuition had to be brought into play. I think this has been one of my driving forces in helping me maintain a real continuing interest in this work. Every time I have discovered a clue from the written history, it always seems to lead me to other related bits of my family history. I felt I must find the Eleanor that I felt the most drawn to. I had to fit that Eleanor into the time frame and place I had dreamed about in this series of these dreams.

I felt like a total novice when I first found myself entwined in this sort of task. I seemed to have been thrown into it whether I was ready for it or not. In my regular life, I would not have had any wish to pursue a project such as this. It had never crossed my mind. Even if I had wanted to write an historical novel, I certainly wouldn't have chosen to write about this particular part of history.

My sister knew I was working on this project and gave me a very timely gift. She sent me a history volume entitled *History of the Kings & Queens of England* by the modern historian David Williamson. That volume has become an extremely valuable resource to use in this undertaking. The Koneckys, the publishers of this history, have been gracious to me and for that I am grateful. In fact, this particular volume is one of the few resources that would even mention Lady Eleanor Talbot-Butler's name and confirm she did exist in the period of history my dreams are centered in.[3]

I was thrilled when I finally began to find little bits of information about her but the history resources were very few. At first I felt all I needed was one believable source. I was amazed that I could have these dreams and then find the same people in the history of the world I am living in now. Then I knew for sure I was on the right course. I couldn't believe I would ever think so but this was exciting history for me now. That thought has kept me working on this even when I get tired of it.

I knew then there was something there to build a story around. Lady Eleanor is one of the main characters my dreams were concerned with. One of the strangest feelings of all is I had never heard of her until these dreams happened! Now the knowledge of her occupies many of my waking hours. This was the key encouragement now for me to want to pursue this research to its conclusion, if there was one to be found.

Lady Eleanor's short life of only thirty years had seriously affected the lives of three consecutive kings. They were, in order, Edward IV, Richard III, and Henry VII. I have found in my research that she was a pivotal character in this whole period of English history. Three kings, each in there own turn, tried arduously to erase the remembrance of her whole being totally from their history forever. This is what finally compelled me to recognize her importance in history and find the proper place for her to be recognized in that history once again, in a positive way.

If I hadn't been able to find what I was looking for when I did, I do not believe I would have gone any further with this project. If I had known how long it would take me to do the research, I don't know if I would have even started it. I have found though, the urge to work on this project seems to come in waves. Every time I have found a contradiction in the written history I have been working with, it has been like the proverbial "hay on the pole" to keep the horses moving. I think one of the main compelling forces with this project that has held my attention so steadfastly was the oddity of this encounter.

The historical contradictions I have just mentioned have served me well. When I first found what I believed to be an historical contradiction, I would wonder why the history was being written that way. Then I would pass it off as the writer or historian not knowing their subject very well or maybe they were just not very good historians. After I started encountering these flaws more regularly, it started to bother me as a novice historical writer. I never had read so much history after university because most of it I found so boring.

The part of this history I couldn't understand was that if certain British historians didn't believe the precontract marriage between Lady Eleanor and Edward IV ever existed, why did so many act as though Lady Eleanor herself never existed either, or at least they gave the impression that they wished it so anyway.[4]

My only saving grace here was to go on and focus on some of these pieces of history that seemed to be contradictions. In the period of history I am writing about, I only have time to touch on them here but I would encourage future historians to read their areas of historical focus very carefully. All the while, I would encourage watching for the blatant historical contradictions that may be encountered in their various fields of study. This is one of the only ways of keeping the true history from becoming political propaganda or just plain lies.

The five Eleanors in the English and French history which I found that might fit the character of the person in my dream, in historical order, were Eleanor of Aquitaine, Eleanor of Brittany, Eleanor of Province, Eleanor of Castile and finally, Lady Eleanor Butler née Talbot. The name Eleanor has certainly proved to be a very popular name in this period of history.

Eleanor of Aquitaine was the first of the five Eleanors. I took a close look in my research to try to find the character of my dreams. The right Eleanor had to fit the right time period, the right ruler period, and the right political party period. I hadn't realized I had to pay such close attention to every minute detail I could remember from the dreams. I will be able to explain later on how I had to use the details I was given to center in on a real person in history to fit the main character in my dreams. Eleanor of Aquitaine comes into the history in the mid-11th century.

Another Eleanor was known as Duchess Eleanor and had married Henry II in 1152. She was heiress to the duchy of Aquitain. Henry was born in Le Mans and he spent his early years in the county of Anjou. Henry's mother was related to William the Conqueror.[5]

David Williamson, the British historian, wrote in his publication *History of the Kings & Queens of England*: "Richard Lionheart, (Richard I), was the third son and fourth child of Henry II and Eleanor. He was born in September 1172. On hearing of his father's death Richard returned to England and was crowned at Westminster Abbey on 3 September 1189. In March 1189, Richard besieged the town of Chalus in Limousin. While riding before the town walls one morning, Richard was struck on the right shoulder by an arrow from a cross-bowman and gangrene set in. Richard died on 6 April 1199, tenderly nursed by his mother. Queen Eleanor lived on for many years and died at Fontevrault on 31 March or 1 April 1204, aged about 82." The timing for Queen Eleanor here is from about 1150 to the early 1200s. I felt his history did not seem close to the timing of my dreams.

Now I began to use my method of historical elimination. Then I was able to move on to the next Eleanor in line, Eleanor of Brittany. As I carried on my research, I found an Eleanor who was known as The Pearl of Brittany. This Eleanor was the daughter of a man named Geoffrey, who was the older brother of King John. The main point here is Eleanor of Aquitaine was the grandmother of Eleanor of Brittany.[6]

"The Pearl of Brittany" or Eleanor of Britany was imprisoned at Bristol Castle, where she was maintained until her death some forty years later, into the reign of Henry III. Eleanor was kept alive under what was called "house arrest" for at least forty years. That was said to be because she was the granddaughter of Eleanor of Aquitaine.

Moving along now, the next Eleanor I came to was Eleanor of Province. Again, historian David Williamson says of her: "She was married to Henry III at Canterbury Cathedral, January 1236, the second daughter and co-heiress of Raymond Beringer V, Count of Province. She was crowned at Westminster Abbey, and although a woman of great beauty and a faithful and devoted wife to the equally faithful Henry III, rendered herself unpopular by her extravagance and her procurement of great offices for her maternal uncles Peter and Boniface of Savoy, the latter of whom became Archbishop of Canterbury."

Henry III died in November 1272. Queen Eleanor exercised the regency until her son, Edward I, returned from the Crusades in 1274. Six years later she retired to the Benedictine Convent at Amesbury, where she took the veil after obtaining the Pope's permission to return her dower. She died there on 24 January 1291, aged 68.

The next Eleanor that I considered is Eleanor of Castile. Historians had commented that she had endured at least sixteen pregnancies in her lifetime. She died on 24 November 1290.[7]

Once again I find in all the research I have done for this section of the history of the life of Edward I and Eleanor of Castile, I found nothing that would make me believe that this Eleanor was the Eleanor of my dreams. Edward I, who died in 1307, was not a fitting image I had formed of the Edward in the dreams. No information I found of this period of history came close to what I was looking for.

So then I moved on to the fifth and final Eleanor. In studying a book by British historian, Alison Weir, I learned that King Edward IV had married a woman named Elizabeth Woodville. I also learned that some historians at this time had said Edward's and Elizabeth's marriage was invalid because Edward IV, at the same time he had married Elizabeth Woodville, was already married to Lady Eleanor Talbot-Butler.

When I read this, I knew I had arrived at what I was looking for. I was overjoyed. My wife was in the same room with me when I found this information. I fell back in my chair and let out a low yell that frightened her. She asked, "Did you find her?" I replied with a loud, "Yes, I certainly did!" I felt my great search was finally over but in fact it was only starting. Still, I was extremely happy. This was the first time I had seen her name in the printed history of England, but that was enough for me to realize I had the beginning proof I needed to show me this was the "woman of my dreams."

Therefore, Edward and Elizabeth's two sons and even their young daughter, Elizabeth, who would eventually marry Henry VII, were labeled as bastards and incapable of inheriting the throne. Richard, Duke of Gloucester, now saw an opening to become the next king of England.[8]

I finally found a copy of the original *Titulus Regius* and I saw Lady Eleanor Butler's name printed as "Dame Elianor Butteler." This woman's name was recorded to be linked to Edward IV. She was also described in that Act as the daughter of John Talbot, Earl of Shrewsbury (1388–1453). This was the second time I would find the "woman of my dreams."

An account of the precontract story was documented by a French historian, Philippe de Commines. He stated the precontract marriage had taken place *c.* 1471. Robert Stillington, Bishop of Bath and Wells had spoken with the Duke of Gloucester, Richard, and said he had performed the precontract ceremony to marry his brother, Edward, to a woman named Lady Eleanor Butler née Talbot. Commines says the Bishop gave proof of the marriage to the government. At that time in England, a precontract marriage was legal but could only be broken by the church. In 1330 an existing precontract with one partner barred marriage to another and was sufficient to bastardize any children of that marriage.[9]

Lady Eleanor was described in *Titulus Regis* as the daughter of John Talbot, Earl of Shrewsbury (1388–1453). Her date of birth is recorded as 1435. In 1449–50 she was married to a Sir Thomas Butler (or Boteler), the son and heir of Ralph, Lord Sudeley, and they went to live at Sudeley Castle in Winchcombe, Gloucestershire.[10]

At this juncture, I want to discuss the Act, *Titulus Regius*. It is one of the most important official government documents of the history of

England. I consider it timely in that it proves Lady Eleanor, or Dame Elianor Butteler, was in fact married to Edward IV. Now, Edward, while still married to Lady Eleanor had married one Elizabeth Woodville in 1464.[11]

The Duke of Gloucester, later to be Richard III, Edward's brother had it passed around that Edward IV's marriage to Elizabeth Woodville was invalid because he had at that time was married to Lady Eleanor; the children born to Elizabeth, Edward's second wife, were bastards and incapable of inheriting the throne. It was then that the Duke of Gloucester saw what might be his only chance to finally become the King of England. After Edward died suddenly at only 41 years old, Richard wasted no time starting his bid for the kingship.

Some historians have said of these claims, that any marriage that didn't have a witness or witnesses could not be legal and binding before the law. So then the logical conclusion that must follow would be that a precontract marriage is just that—it is not legally considered a marriage.

A little known fact that I found was that Edward IV had lived with Elizabeth Woodville for nineteen years and that issue was never brought before the courts of England before Richard III would make his bid for kingship.[12]

After the death of Edward IV, in the spring of 1483, the Duke of Gloucester then declared Edward's two sons and daughter, bastards and legally not fit to rule. Edward and Elizabeth's two sons soon disappeared. Then the Duke of Gloucester was declared Richard III, King of England.

In 1484, the Act, *Titulus Regius*, was passed, setting out Richard's title to the throne. Richard III was not king very long. He was killed at the Battle of Bosworth Field in 1485 by the troops of Henry VII.

In November 1485 Henry VII wanted *Titulus Regius* to be deleted from the Statute Books. The Parliament Roll of 1484 was suppressed and all official documents referring to the Act, destroyed. Anyone having a copy of the *Titulus Regius* had to give it to the Lord Chancellor by Easter 1486 or they could be arrested and imprisoned and fined.

I discovered in my research, that the name of the child of Eleanor's was first known as Giles Gurney. However, in my first dream a man by that name was the butler to Lady Eleanor at Sudeley Castle. He had taken that position in 1452. In the dreams, he was of Jewish/Moorish decent and had changed his name from Rubin Manni to Giles Gurney. Rubin Manni, alias Giles Gurney, was supposedly from Acre, in Israel. When he was 25 years old, he made his way to the Island of Cyprus. Then, sometime later got on a merchant ship and went to the Island of Menorca and debarked at the port of Mao. From there he went to France and then to England. As he was trained as a tailor when he was a young man, he was able to get employment right away making clothes for wealthy people in London. Rubin Manni knew from the history, the English had come to Jerusalem and Acre, during the Crusades and had started referring to themselves as Kings of Jerusalem. He was also aware, that during the coronation of King Richard I, Jews in London and several other towns were forbidden to attend the coronation and some massacres followed.

That is why Rubin Manni changed his name and learned to speak Italian and English before he went to England. Giles Gurney was the person whom I believe buried Jane de Wigmore's baby boy in the garden on the north-west corner of Sudeley Castle. In the same place he buried Lady Eleanor when she passed away from starvation. He was told to bury her quickly so no one would see her body or know anything about what had happened. That took place in late June after young Edward de Wigmore had secretly visited his mom.

Shortly after that, Giles Gurney had to leave Sudeley in a real hurry, under threat of death, because now he was privy to too much damaging information. No one knew where he went or anything about him after that.

What really bothered me now, at this point in my research, was that it seemed that simple logic had been thrown out the window. Then the more I considered all the points of reasoning here, the more I was left in disbelief.

The more information I had been blessed with, the more I could see why people in political control at this period of time in the history, were saying and doing as they wished! Those who were supporting the power structure of the time were laying down a purposely confusing "blanket of truth." Much of the historical facts of the Middle Ages era are still not known today.

In conclusion of this part of the story, I have found this endeavor to be an eye-opening experience on many levels. I don't believe the truth has been told about Lady Eleanor Talbot-Butler yet, but I am hoping this publication will change all that.

I am aware that some historians have discovered this person and have written some kind and interesting comments about her. Purposely, I have refrained from researching any of the new works that may have been published about her so their writing would not influence mine.

For me, as I have said before, the most phenomenal aspect of this whole story has been to have had a dream about this person, Lady Eleanor, whom I had no idea even existed, and then start collecting information about her. Another aspect I find so interesting is I feel emotionally attached but yet very comfortable in finding information and writing about her. I have now discovered that the Talbot family, Eleanor's branch, is married into my Paget family line!

I really believe that these dreams I have had are not just random occurrences. I think I have had windows opened into other relevant realms that I have been a distinct part of in my past. I now have more of an urge to see this project through. I feel now, the findings magnify themselves in all the valid connections I have discovered. This task has compelled me to want to see Lady Eleanor in a much brighter aspect and I want to make her a larger part of my family history as well as this history in general.

It is my hope that historians writing of this period of history will try to include some information about Lady Eleanor Talbot-Butler in the future. So far, I have discovered her as a beautiful, intelligent and personable being. She was feared and destroyed by powerful and desperate, misguided people, who never tried to understand her. Now I can recognize her as a part of my life! I remain extremely proud to have come to know about her, and to realize she is one of my dearest ancestors!

A good friend has painted a portrait of Lady Eleanor based on my descriptions of her from my dreams of when she had gone to meet with Edward IV to try to get him to return Sudeley Castle and the manor houses to her. This portrait of Lady Eleanor illustrates the cover of this book.

CHAPTER TWELVE
The Structure Of The Dreams

I was surprised when I learned in the dreams that young Edward had been adopted by Jane de Wigmore. I was more surprised to learn in my recent research that young Edward was known by historians as de Wigmore soon after he was born. I have now found records of his birth that prove his name was given as Edward de Wigmore. His birth is registered as 1467 or 1468. All the records I have found show he died in infancy, except one that states that a member of his family line, Richard Wigmore, went on to serve in the government of Elizabeth I.[1]

I don't know who named this child but I don't believe King Edward himself would have named him. The most interesting fact here for me is the father of this male child is stated to be King Edward IV Plantagenet, King of England. I believe young Edward was named after King Edward was already dead. I don't believe Edward would have wanted to name his son after a woman's family who had taken him and hidden him away. He showed his frustration by trying to destroy Jane de Wigmore's family castle. Edward, in my view, wasn't the least bit concerned as to what the child's name was; he went to de Wigmore Castle looking for him to have him put away or killed. He already had two other sons by his second marriage, which he believed he could pass his kingship to; he didn't need another one. Edward IV died in 1483 at the age of only 41. This fact would arouse my imagination but I knew I couldn't pursue any research on it now.

If young Edward de Wigmore was born in c1467, that would have made him 16 years old when Edward died. Edward IV was 19 when he became king. I am not sure who named Lady Eleanor's son in the actual history, but in the dreams that was decided by both Jane and Eleanor when he was taken to live with Jane. Some kings had inherited their kingship when they were too young to rule. In such a case a family member, or a person designated by the government, would be appointed as protector of the king to run the government in the king's stead until it was believed the king was capable of running the government on his own. When Edward IV died, his young son Edward V was only twelve years old. Later in this publication, I explain the course of events that would decide who would be the protector for young Edward V as he was only 12 years old when his father Edward IV died.[2]

In the first dream when Lady Eleanor explained to young Edward that he had been adopted by Jane, that really struck a chord with me. I quickly made a mental note and then put it out of my thoughts at that time. I could barely keep up with what was happening in the dream as it was. I was so new at this kind of experience I had to focus all my attention just on the movement of the dreams unfolding.

Some time later, I thought about the adoption that took place in the dreams again. I thought about what caused me to mentally react so strongly when that was mentioned in the first dream. As I considered that idea later I realized that when I was five and six years old, I had crying spells at night. My mother used to hear me crying in my sleep and she would come and gently wake me to ask why I was crying. I would tell her it was because I felt I had been adopted when I was very young. She would always tell me she was my only mother. I always took comfort in that and would go back to sleep. After I turned seven years old, I didn't have those adoption dreams or the crying spells anymore. I forgot all about them, until I started having this series of dreams and was reminded of that experience.

I began to wonder if health and emotional problems we might have had in some of our past lives could be passed from one life to another. I realize now that my dreams of being adopted rang a bell for me in my present life. I wondered if these dreams were happening to let me know how certain events carry over from lifetime to lifetime.

In *The New Beginning*, the first chapter of this book, I explained how I felt when I realized subconsciously that a dream was occurring and I was totally immersed in it. This re-occurred throughout the dreams, in all parts of them including subsequent fragments of the dreams. This is where I got the idea to entitle this book *A Dream Within A Dream*. In these dreams, I also felt as though I was watching myself and the events happening around me, but I didn't feel as though I was taking part in any of the activities. That was fine by me because I just wanted to watch what was being presented. I felt more like a by-stander, watching a play taking place all around me, at first. In this sequence of dreaming, the whole while, I kept having an urgent feeling that I must pay close attention to what was happening. I did have a lot of doubt at the beginning of this long journey.[3]

Intermittently, I would have pressing and fearful feelings. They were random type feelings never caused by the same issues. These were often questionings such as *When will this be over?*, *Why am I so involved here?* or *Where is the exit?* At times I would have feelings that I had better "watch my back," as the saying goes. At other times I was fascinated by my seeming awareness in the dreams.

My ability to reason seemed to have matured to a level somewhat beyond what I thought I was capable of in my normal life. There was no one there to judge me but me and it was good to feel that much freedom. I don't believe we realize how much conscious value we place on wanting people to like us.

At the beginning of the first dream, I felt the most vacillation of consciousness. I felt strongly that I was moving in and out of a present life reality and ever deeper into a past life reality. I was aware that I was afraid of this dream. This was all such new territory for me. I felt as though I was in some uncharted waters. Even so, the dreams were extremely vivid.

As the first dream sequence continued, I began to feel I was starting to play an ever increasingly, important role in them. At some point, near the first realization that I was involved in these dreams, I began to define my role more aggressively. I felt, for the first time in the dreams, I really needed to be there to try in some way to remember and record what was taking place. I wasn't witnessing just random acts, there was a story being told and I realized I should pay close attention and try to remember as much of it as I could.

I experienced a feeling that I could see myself looking through a hole or opening. Then I realized I was seeing the inside of a castle. Now my subconscious mind was beginning to click in. I surprised myself with being able to reason so linearly in my dream state, even though I tend not to be so structured when I'm awake. I didn't appreciate that I was going through such a linear process at first but then I realized I had been doing this in my dream states, not so much in the first dream but more so in the later three dreams.[4]

I felt I had a new tool to work with. I thought it would help me better understand the different parts of what I had experienced in this new set of dreams. I also realized that after the first dream, I did feel more comfortable during the new sequence of dreams I was now writing about. I had made a conscious choice to not only look through the hole I had seen in my first dream but to also be willing to stay with the dream on to a further state. I didn't realize until after the first dream, I didn't have to look through any more holes to carry on the rest of the subsequent dreams. Now I felt I had made a big step to become interactive with the events and characters I encountered in the remaining three dreams. I felt now I wasn't so afraid of these dreams.

Now I began to see a pattern forming. In the dreams I had experienced so far, when I began to get into situations which I may have felt uncomfortable in, I would want to make a "run for it" and change the dream or stop it altogether. Still, I was making a conscious choice by deciding whether I wanted to participate or not. I never realized I had that choice before. I was confronted with making many decisions in these dreams. I knew I had become more interactive with them.

I recall the first dream though, being so powerful I don't know even now if I could have stopped that dream if had wanted to. The ending of it was a blur. It just seemed to fade away. The ending was unclear. I don't remember mentally stopping it. I think it ended because I was mentally and physically drained. It had covered so much material. I was still in a state of shock from witnessing such an invasive and novel experience.

Later on after the first dream I believed I was on to something very important. I believed there was something happening in it I could use as a mental tool. I began to believe it was a product or a conglomeration of all the past lives I may have lived. I believe now, this process can leave us with many thoughts and feelings. For some of us, I believe we know how our dreams can become a valuable part of our consciousness if we are not afraid to experience them.

Publishers have asked me, when I told them I was writing this book, if it was fact or fiction. I explained to them that I had discovered a woman in my dreams that I had never heard of or knew anything about, and then I had found her documented in historical publications. I do not consider the parts of my dreams that have been corroborated by the historical record to be fiction! However, I am not claiming that my manuscript is wholly factual since both the dreams and the historical record leave blanks in the puzzle that I have attempted to fill.

I don't believe our dreams are all fact or fiction but again maybe that is why they are called dreams. Our dreams are not considered real anyway. I'll let the critics decide whether my manuscript is fact or fiction or both. I just want to write the story of all four of these dreams as they took place, as close as I am able, from the first time I became aware of them in my consciousness.[5]

In this manuscript, King Edward IV, King Richard III and King Henry VII did not see "Dame Eleanor Butler" as a figment of their imaginations, after they had witnessed her name imprinted in one of the most famous legal documents of English history, the *Titulus Regius*.

Richard used as a threat the fact that, while he was still married to Lady Eleanor Butler, Edward IV had married Elizabeth Woodville and fathered three children, said to be bastards. Richard was preparing to use this bit of information as a tool for making sure no one else was in his way when he made his play for the throne.

Later on, when Henry VII became king, he would want any mention of or about Lady Eleanor Talbot-Butler, to be collected and burned, forever to clear the way for him to his throne. They both, Richard and Henry, tried ardently to erase all memory of her ever being in this world. That is why I am spending such long hours on this project. I want to find out and solve this centuries-old mystery of why Lady

Eleanor Talbot-Butler was so important to have been left out of most of the printed works of history ever published from that era to the present time.

The historian George Buck in the late 1600s, found a copy of the "Croyland Chronicle," showing an original copy of the *Titulus Regius* (also known as the *Act of Settlement*) that had been preserved and it was finally revealed to the public in print. Henry VII was worried he might not make it to the throne in 1485 even though the Act had been suppressed. The problem was that the woman Henry wanted to marry was Edward IV's daughter Elizabeth, who had been accused of being a bastard along with her two brothers, as I have discussed before.[6] The historian David Williamson explains how this situation was remedied by the *Act of Legitimization*[7] which legitimized their marriage.

The intensity of all this material and how it had to fit into place has become a real mystery and a life challenge. However, I'm beginning to see this as something that is of extreme historical importance. I knew the time had come to do this and I knew I had to get as much of it written down as I could while I still had the memory of all the dreams fresh in my mind. I was worried that some of the most important parts of that history could easily be overlooked and not included. I believed I had already seen that to be the case too many times in my research so far and I didn't want to see that happen any more. I have only been able to present as much information as I could to correspond with the material found in the dreams. This has helped me present what I believe is a readable manuscript for publication.

Another characteristic that I observed that was consistent throughout all of the dreams was that, once I began a dream, nothing interrupted the focus of that process. I may have awakened from dream one earlier than I wanted to because I was so uncomfortable by the time the dream finished. The shock of all of a sudden being confronted with a blatant rush of history from 500 years ago gave me a lot to consider. Then having to try to jot down some notes, which I tried but was too shaken to write, was quite an event, I shall not easily forget. I carried this event around in my head for months before I could even approach it in any form.

I couldn't understand why the dream kept hounding me. I just wanted to forget it and go back to sleep. It seemed I was being encouraged from a hidden force to take part in this. It was as though it was trying to show me something I wasn't even sure I was interested in. It was as though I began to pay attention to what was happening just to get it to leave me alone.

In the other three dreams, I knew sort of what to expect when they started. I was able to recognize soon after they began, that they were the same kind of dream and subject matter as the first dream. With the remaining three dreams the endings were about the same. The endings just slowly faded out into nothing and I was able to realize the dream was ending. They all started much the same way. The great intensity of the first dream was not quite so present in the three later dreams. The overall format for the dreams remained much the same in all four dreams. I had established enough of a mental outline of the first dream so that allowed me to pick up where I left off as they proceeded.

Once I became familiar with the dreams and what the general plot was, I began to enjoy the story even more. With the more tragic parts of the first dream, I learned from my research what parts of the subsequent dreams that I had to grasp. I somehow knew that I had to pay very close attention to the events I was witnessing in order to fill in any blank spots that were occurring. I must admit, as I have said before, I wasn't familiar with any of this part of English history at all.

At this time, I want to point out that I am beginning to believe that one of the purposes of dreaming is to show us our most dominant personal traits as we view them, good or bad. On a personal note here, I have always seen myself as a person who was willing to aid anyone who might need help in any way. I think though, there may be a certain amount of ego involved here as well, in the sense of perhaps wanting to see one's self as a hero.

I remember thinking in the dream that here young Edward was only six or seven years of age. He was truly frightened when he was warned not to be concerned with the person upstairs because he could be in a lot of danger if he tried to help her. His immediate reaction to what he had just been told was to take that as a direct threat to his survival. In the actual history the tall bodyguard turned out to be Sir James Tyrrell, a main character in William Shakespeare's *Richard III*.[8]

As the dream proceeded young Edward couldn't see the man anymore because he was temporally surrounded and blinded by a bright ray of sunlight. I see that scene as a sign that Young Edward had seen the light and he wasn't afraid anymore. Symbolically, as I see this, he was surrounded by the light to protect himself. He could recall being able to hear the man's hard-healed boots still clacking on the big stone floor as he was left standing there in a seemingly helpless state. Now, I didn't realize when I wrote down the phrase "seemingly helpless state," that young Edward might have wanted the big man to think he was helpless. I think he actually reasoned that maybe the tall man wouldn't be so concerned about him and send someone to keep an eye on him. I think he just wanted to be forgotten altogether. That way he could still go upstairs to see if he could help the person up there who he thought needed some kind of help.

This above scene helped me realized why I have always been so interested in helping other people instead of getting other people to help me. As a child I was small, skinny and not very strong. I had asthma when I was ten. I think that is why, as I got older, I had developed a sense of superiority from being able to help people. I have always felt vulnerable in having to ask for help because it made me feel helpless.

Another interesting point here for me is I want to call attention to the idea of how active my mind was in the dream state. I realized I was thinking while I was dreaming. I know we must be thinking when we are dreaming because how else would we be able to store and remember our dreams. Then remembering is also another clue to the fact that our memory function is responding to the dreaming. My locution skills were at a peak in the later three dreams but not the first dream. In that dream I was experiencing the raw story and I had no facts to compare anything to. I had no idea what the dream was all about then. As I learned what this story was about I became more relaxed and paid closer attention to what was happening and why.

The thought that caught my attention in this part of the dreaming was that I really reacted to the threat young Edward had encountered in the first dream. After the tall soldier had told him not to go up to see the person that was crying upstairs, young Edward had acted as though he could see himself from above and he was smiling. He acted as though he wasn't defeated. Instead he showed a sense of strength and looked much older, taller and stronger to me.

Further, he seemed to have been overcome by a sudden urge to take the tall man's warning not as a threat but as a challenge. The voice crying from upstairs had changed in pitch and the person up there seemed now only to be calling out for him to come to her. Somehow he now had a kind of special connection with her, whoever she was. Her calling out to him was like a signal she was sending to connect with him only. He seemed to take great pride in that.

In order for me to understand and be able to pass on to the readers the story of my life changing dreams, I had to study what some of the more up-to-date authors had to say about dreams and dreaming.

When I began researching the information I could find on that subject, I started finding such terms as "interdimensional portals," "time traveler's portals," "past life regression" and "lucid dreaming."[9] These were some of the terms I wanted to find out the characteristics of. I read about reincarnation and personal growth. A very important part for me in this writing was when I read about how past life fragments can be mixed into our dreams. Right away I felt that was exactly what had been happening in my dreams, especially in the first dream and to a lesser extent in the other three dreams.[10]

I had never heard of or read any of this work on dreaming before I had my dreams. I learned that it was very important to be able to recall your dreams. When the first dream began, I woke up with a jolt, almost as though I had just been dropped back to earth from the sky. I have no way of knowing how long I had been in a solid dream state.[11]

I believe I have gone through the portals that were mentioned in the books on dreaming. Another very important lesson I learned was to not be afraid to go back to your dreams. I was afraid after the first dream to go into the second dream when it started. After the second dream started though, I seemed to have more control of what I thought I might be able to learn from that experience.

Young Edward asked questions in the dreams and he was amazed at what the characters he was interacting with would tell him. Also, I can find my answers in the history books more easily now it seems because I know more about what I am looking for. I know some of the people that will read this book might say, *How is it possible to go back to a dream you have had and dream parts you may want to go over again?*

Lucid dreaming is described in my research as a state in dreaming in which the dreamer can definitely recognize that they are dreaming. Dreams such as these seem as real and vivid as conscious reality. Also the senses of sound, sight, taste, and smell seem intensified. The books I have researched on dreaming have also explained, that to remember your dreams, you want to see them as important and that they have a value as being from your subconscious mind. Your dreams are about you.

Lucid dreams are believed to stay in the memory for a longer time. I believe these dreams I had were lucid dreams or I may not have been able to remember them for such a long time and I still can see the images from these four dreams vividly. I do believe this is true because I can still refer to all four dreams and that has helped me enlarge the experience of this whole story.[12]

Based on what I learned about dreaming, I believed I had experienced lucid dreaming because I could see and feel the energy of the characters I was encountering in the dreams as if I was actually there. I could see vividly what was occurring out in the front fields at Sudeley Castle. The sounds in my dreams were as clear as when awake. The sound of the woman crying upstairs was very audible. Although I'm somewhat hard of hearing while awake, at times within the dreams, my hearing seemed to have improved a bit because so many of the sounds I heard were strikingly clear. My sense of taste and smell were also heightened. I could taste the good pea soup and bread the young Edward was given at Lorne's farm. I could feel the clear cold water he drank from some of the streams he crossed in his travels. As for smell, his and my sense of smell became the strongest when he made it upstairs where his mother was being held.

As he entered the chamber room in the front corner tower he couldn't believe the smell. She couldn't wash her body or her clothes and her toilet was a hole in the floor. He remembered feeling extremely sick and he thought he was going to throw-up but he didn't, out of respect for the woman in the room. He didn't know she was his mother at first but that didn't matter at the time. He addressed her with good manners and she did him as well. Every time I think of that scene, I have many mixed emotions; even though this was only a dream, that really made an impression on me. It still conjures up resentful feelings of disgust just to see any human treated that way by anyone. Everything in the dreams was in color, the same as in real life. Edward had a sharp memory of the metal of the soldiers armor that was so bright it blinded him to look at it in the full sunlight.[13]

Other dreaming-related material that I read mentioned "subconscious recognition." I interpreted that term to mean that something like a déjà vu can come about through a past life connection with certain people or even places. A recognition such as this can be immediate and manifested clearly as an attraction or repulsion, each in varying degrees. This also could be brought on by even a repetition of behaviors from a past life.[14]

When I started recalling the story of my first dream, I felt hopelessly alone. I didn't know where it had come from. Later, as I thought about feeling that way, I recalled that even when I was a child I used to spend a lot of time alone. I didn't give aloneness much thought. I always viewed loneliness a lot differently than what I called "aloneness."

Loneliness was like sadness to me as a child, and it still is. I didn't ever mind aloneness, even as a child, because it gave me time to be alone with my own thoughts. Most of the time when I would go out to explore new environments or to just go for a walk, my dog was always with me. I would talk to my dog just like another person anyway. She never talked back but I knew she understood me. When we moved out to the country when I was in grade school, I was with children my own age all day. I was always glad to get home so I could be quiet for awhile or just play ball with a few of my neighbor friends.

I thought I might have been a hermit sometime back in the past. Later on in studying my family I believe some men and women in the old country were recluses or hermits. I thought that was a normal response since in my whole first dream, young Edward was only a child but he spent most of his time in these dreams not really knowing who his mother or his father were. He was always with someone who was a surrogate person to him. Even so, he never seemed to mind being alone and loneliness didn't seem to be a part of his character. In the dreams, because he was so preoccupied with just keeping up with what was happening, he didn't ever seem too lonely. He had times when he could have been lonely and sad but he didn't seem to take time to linger on it. He was with people who cared for him and that he respected and loved.

When I finally did start writing down the details of what I could remember from the first dream, I surprised myself that I could remember so much. The hardest part of getting started writing down all the details I could remember from these dreams, was the parts where I felt what I was experiencing was more of a nightmare than a dream. Then I realized what I had experienced was the most different kind of dream I had ever had. Some parts of the dream I shunned because they were frighting; even in my adult mind I didn't want to recall them. I admit I had to wait awhile before I could or even wanted to recall them because they were so painful and sad in places.

I discovered another piece of information that described our dreaming as not just having dreams. It is not imagining or wishing or day dreaming. We can recognize and describe them but we don't know how to apply them. One piece I found that I think describes how we dream says: "In our dreams we only see what we already believe and that helps to confirm our view of the world."

I see this collection of dreams as my own tiny video library. It didn't come complete with instant replay but the recall came when I needed it the most. I didn't have to program these dreams because they were such an unusual event in my life. There is no way I would have been interested in this area of history anyway. Still, they have remained constantly in my mental focus and the information in them is now embedded in my psyche. These dreams are as clear to me now as they were when they first came to me.

After the shock of the first dream had begun to subside the other dreams seemed to fit into their own natural occurrence. Every dream seemed to be an extended review of the preceding one all in their own order. Since my experiencing the fourth and final dream in this series of dreams, I have not had any dreams that could be related to these. In fact, I have not had any dreams that would even begin to come close to the intensity of these dreams. I am satisfied now that I have completed this past life review, if in fact that is what it was. I feel grateful to have been given the opportunity to be made aware that my life had more than one dimension to it. Maybe there is more of these dreams for me out there somewhere.

Most of my life, I have been aware that many peoples believe this life we are living now is the only life we will ever live. I believed that too, until I had these dreams.

CHAPTER THIRTEEN
Edward IV: His Private Wars

T he first reign of Edward IV as King of England was from 1461 to 1471. He sat with his first Parliament when he was just 19 years old. The British historian David Williamson, in his publication *History of the Kings & Queens of England*, gives us a step-by-step description of Edward IV's path to glory.

> Edward was the second son, an older brother Henry having died in infancy, of Richard, 3rd Duke of York, and his wife Cecily, the twelfth and youngest daughter of Ralph Neville, 1st Earl of Westmoreland, both parents descending from Edward III. He was born at Rouen, France, where his father was stationed on official duties, on 28 August 1442.
>
> As soon as they were of an age to do so, Edward and his next brother, Edmund, took up arms in the Yorkist cause. In December of 1460 Edward succeeded as the 4th Duke of York. On the 4th March 1461, Henry VI was deposed and Edward was declared King in Parliament. He was crowned at Westminster Abbey on 29 June.
>
> On 1 May 1464 Edward was married at the parish church of Grafton Regis, Northhamptonshire. His bride was Elizabeth, a lady some five years his senior and the widow of Sir John Grey. He was killed at the battle of St. Albans in 1461. Her father, Richard Woodville, later to be

ennobled as Earl Rivers, was a country gentleman of an undistinguished family, but her mother was Jacquette of Luxembourg, the widow of John, Duke of Bedford, fourth son of Henry IV. ... The marriage to a lady of comparatively humble birth with such strong Lancastrian connections caused grave offense to Edward's brothers and other members of the court when it was presented to them as a fait accompli some months after it had taken place. Nevertheless, the new queen was crowned at Westminster Abbey with considerable pomp on 26 May 1465. The stately and aloof Elizabeth, who was already the mother of two sons by her first husband, presented the king with ten children, three sons and seven daughters. ...

The king's marriage had caused Warwick "the King Maker" to switch his allegiance to the Lancastrians and re-open the civil war. After defeating Edward near Banbury in 1469, he went to France to raise more troops and returned to effect the "re-adaptation" of Henry VI, forcing Edward to flee to France and the pregnant Queen Elizabeth and her children to seek Sanctuary at Westminster. The tables were turned in 1471 when Edward returned, and the slaying of Warwick at the battle of Barnet, followed soon after the battle of Tewkesbury and the deaths of Henry VI and his son, put an end to Lancastrian hopes.

Edward's brother George, Duke of Clarence, had sided with his father-in-law, Warwick, and, although he changed sides again, was finally convicted of high treason and confined to the Tower of London, where he met his death in 1478, supposedly drowned in a butt of malmsey wine. How far Edward and his youngest brother, Richard, Duke of Gloucester, were implicated in his death is not known.

Edward was a popular and pleasure-loving monarch, eating and drinking to excess and then taking emetics so that he might start again. He had all the makings of a ruthless despot, however, and had he lived longer he might have become one of the most powerful English kings.

Historian David Williamson elsewhere explains: "The eldest son of Edward IV and Elizabeth Woodville was born at Westminster on 4 November 1470, at a time when his father was in exile in Burgundy and his mother and her children had sought refuge in Sanctuary. In a few months all had changed and Edward was back on the throne and able to create his son Prince of Wales and Earl of Chester, Duke of Cornwall, Earl of March and Earl of Pembrook successively."[1]

Richard of York, Edward IV's father, was a great landowner. In England he owned estates in twenty shires. Edward had the strength of his mother's inheritance. She was an heiress of the Mortimer earls of March. Ludlow Castle was owned by her and became Edward's center of operations.

Edward's mother, Duchess Cecily, was a member of the powerful Neville clan, who had a good understanding of English politics in the 1450s. Edward spent time at Fotheringhay Castle. His brother Richard and perhaps Edward as well were born there.

Windsor Castle held a certain fascination for Edward. He knew his ancestor, Edward III, had founded a secret order there. It was called the "Order of the Garter." It displayed the banners showing the Coats of Arms of all the past knights that had been registered in the Order since it was begun in 1348. These banners were and still are displayed at the Chapel of St. George's within Windsor Castle,[2] as far as I know.

Edward was interested in the "Garter" not just because it was begun by his ancestor but mainly he realized its worth and used membership in it as a diplomatic and political tool. Heads of state were elected into the Order as far back as the late 1300s. Membership during Edward's kingship also included Federigo da Montefeltro, duke of Urbino commander of the papal troops, elected in 1474. Edward's personal favor determined members entry into this powerful order.[3]

Duke Richard of York, Edward's father, had a plan to entrench his political views in Ireland in the mid-1450s. He was able to gain the support of the Anglo-Irish, which then led to victory of the Yorkist in England. In the wake of that success, a famous political family, the

Butlers, were crushed by Edward's first parliament. He had the brothers of Lady Eleanor Talbot arrested on inflated charges and had their properties taken by the crown. Again, this is the family Eleanor Talbot married into.

The Earls of Shrewsbury (the Talbots, Lady Eleanor's family) and the Earls of Wiltshire and Ormond (the Butlers, Lady Eleanor's in-laws) were blamed for many of the failures of the English government.[5] In February 1461, Edward's army fought against Lancasterian forces at Mortimer's Cross, a few miles from Edward's stronghold at de Wigmore Castle. That battle was a victory for the Yorkist and Edward and his troops headed for London where Edward became king.

The Butler Family were an old Anglo-Irish family. Lady Eleanor married Sir Thomas Butler and she was of the Talbot family. These were two very powerful and influential families in Ireland, Wales, and England during the reign of Edward IV. He worked at killing the heads of these families on the battlefield and took their properties away from them and passed the properties on to members of his own family as well to men who had served him in Wales to gain power there. These were part of what I believe was referred to as "Edward's Private Wars."

Edward's victory at Mortimer's Cross brought him a kingship, a lot of personal prestige, and a larger army which followed him to London. They were mostly Yorkist servants and retainers who had come at their own expense. His title to the throne depended on his legitimate inheritance.

A petition from the commons, in Edward's first parliament November 1461, stated his claim that, because the Lancastrian kings had all been usurpers, the right title lay with him as heir of Lionel of Clarence. After his father had died, he thought he should have lawful right to the crown. Edward stated that under the rule of the usurper Henry VI, there was unrest, inward war and trouble and "unrightwiseness."[4]

Edward's Yorkists had to follow the rules of kingship correctly. The ceremonies following Edward's entry into London were carefully stage-managed. The first step was an address by the chancellor, Bishop George Neville, to set out the articles of Edward's title. The populace expressed their wish to have him as their king. This news was brought to Edward at Baynard's Castle, the York family's London house.[5]

In February 1462, Edward was given very large estates in Leicestershire, Lincolnshire and Rutland, from newly forfeited lands of James, Earl of Wiltshire; William, Viscount Beaumont and Thomas, Lord Roos. Further substantial grants of land followed in 1464 and 1469. He received several lands from private persons, then there were his own purchases of property in this area.[6] The dispersal of lands of James Butler, Earl of Wiltshire and Ormond, was begun in November 1461. By August 1462, the Earl's fifty-one manors and lordships in England, spreading over twelve counties from west of England to East Anglia, had been granted to beneficiaries.[7]

David Williamson continues:

> When his father died unexpectedly, the 12-year-old Prince Edward was residing at Ludlow, one of his official residences, and on receiving the news that he was now king, set out for London, to be met on the way at Stony Stratford by his uncle Richard, Duke of Gloucester, on his way down from York. Richard conducted his nephew to London with every sign of loyalty and they were met outside the city by the Lord Mayor and leading citizens, who escorted them to the Tower, which it is alleged the young king never left again.
>
> A sensation was caused some weeks later when Robert Stillington, Bishop of Bath and Wells, and a former Chancellor, who was openly hostile to the Woodvilles, questioned the validity of Edward IV's marriage to Elizabeth. Edward, it was claimed, had been precontracted to Lady Eleanor Butler, widow of Sir Thomas Butler ... and she was still living at the time of Edward's marriage to Elizabeth ... [making the marriage] invalid and their children bastards. It followed that Edward V was no longer king and he was declared deposed on 25 June 1483, his uncle Gloucester being proclaimed as Richard III in his place.[8]

CHAPTER FOURTEEN
Dreams Of The Old Empire

I found some interesting information about the old history of Europe and The House of Plantagenet. I had started researching for more material for this part of my manuscript. I learned how Edward IV, during his time as King of England, had returned this name to the foreground of French and English as well as European political life in general.

Then I started reading about The House of Anjou, which was located in the provincial area by that name in western France. The House of Anjou was associated with a man named Fulques or Fulk IV, the Count of Anjou. He married a woman named Bertrade de Montfort. They had a son who was known as Count Fulk V of Anjou.

Fulk V was born in c1089-1092 in Angers and died in November 1143 in Acre. He was also known as Fulk the Younger and was Count of Anjou from 1109 to 1129. He was King of Jerusalem from 1131 to his death. He was also the paternal grandfather of Henry I of England. In 1092, his mother, Bertrade deserted her husband and bigamously married King Philip I of France.[1]

Fulk V became Count of Anjou when his father died in 1109, at the age of "about" twenty. In that year he married Erembourg of Maine, cementing Angevin or House of Anjou control over the county of Maine. In studying this history, I have learned about a people known as the Salic Franks, that settled into an area of northern France in the 4th century. They developed a legal code which became known as Salic Law. Under these laws, women were excluded from the line of succession to the throne of France.[2] Now, the history I have read stated that Bertrade Montfort had left Fulk IV and bigamously married King Philip I of France in 1092. I believe France at this time in their history was ruled under Salic Law. The law stated: "Any child born into a bigamous relationship would then be considered a bastard and could not rule."

In my studying this history, I found there seemed to be some doubt about the date of Fulk's birth and using the word "about" caught my attention.

The inference here is if Fulk was twenty years old in 1109 when he became Count of Anjou, it would mean he was born in 1089. This began to look like a cover-up to show Fulk was not born in 1092, into a bigamous marriage, when his mother married King Philip I of France.

Assuming Fulk V was born into a bigamous marriage, then it would seem to follow that, under Salic Law, he would then be declared a bastard and should not have been allowed to legally rule. Also, any of his offspring would then be considered bastards as well and could not legally rule.

Another question here is why would the Catholic Church of France ever have sanctioned or declared a bigamous marriage as legal? It seems as though the kings of Jerusalem made up their own laws as they went along. It seems as though England and France were supposedly ignoring Salic Law as that legal system seemed to be declining in prominence at this time. I think that the pressure of the Crusades may have effected this change.

King Baldwin II (of Bouillion) had no male heirs but had already designated his daughter Melisende to succeed him. Baldwin II wanted to marry his daughter to Fulk as he was a wealthy crusader, experienced military commander and a widower.

In England, a king could not marry a widow but I do not yet know how the crown looked at the marriage status of a widower. In France, the right to the throne could not have been held by Melisende because of the Salic Laws. Again, these laws barred women from succeeding or transmitting a claim to the throne. At this time in France (1092), the Salic Laws were in place and were the law of the land! So when Bertrade married King Philip I, Fulk V, by the laws of France at that time, should have been declared a "bastard." This royal line would then have been broken with no male heir to succeed King Baldwin II. Henry II would have had no royal ascent or claim to the House of Anjou. I believe this situation would have also made the royal claims of the House of Plantagenet null and void.

I believe it would follow that Fulk V could not legally have been declared a count or a King of Jerusalem, or anything but a "bastard" in England as well as France. Further, Fulk V, as I understand this research, could not have been of a true Merovingian bloodline because he had his "coronation" to become the King of Jerusalem in 1131. Again, from what I had learned from my studies of the culture of the Merovingians, a true king of the Merovingian bloodline did not need a "coronation" to prove he was a king. A true king would automatically become a king when he turned twelve years old, provided he was of the old bloodline. That tradition did not seem to be a consideration here.[3]

As an aside here, I want to mention that the Merovingian kings had amassed a great amount of wealth. Some of the gold coins they had minted bore the equal-armed cross, representing the Frankish Kingdom of Jerusalem during the Crusades. The Paget coat of arms still bears that equal-armed cross.

That could have weakened Henry's political power as well as his family name. Henry did mend his ways toward Fulk by realizing he could marry his (Fulk's) son, Geoffrey of Anjou, to his daughter, Matilda. There again is another denial of Salic Law. So, the outcome of that marriage is written in the history books as Geoffrey V Plantagenet Count of Anjou and Maine. Their only off-spring was Henry, who became Henry II, King of England. Henry's logic here must have been that he could sweeten the bloodline a little. Again, Merovingian traditions were not popular and or acknowledged in England.

I got another piece of information from *History of the Kings & Queens of England* by David Williamson, that I could not pass up. It stated that "Queen Matilda died at Westminster on 1 May 1118. Two years later, Henry's only legitimate son, William, was drowned crossing the channel from Normandy. In hope of having further legitimate issue, Henry remarried in 1122. His bride was Adeliza, daughter of Godfrey Count of Louvain, but the marriage was childless and in 1126

Henry designated his daughter Matilda, a "widow" of the Emperor Henry V, to be his heir and chose a second husband for her in the person of Geoffrey Plantagenet, son of Fulk, Count of Anjou. Although William and Matilda were Henry's only legitimate offspring, he left a large illegitimate progeny of 21 or more children, among them Robert, Earl of Gloucester, who was to champion his half-sister Matilda in her claim to the throne."[4]. Further, it would again logically follow that if Fulk V had been declared legally a bastard, then his son, Geoffrey, being born in France should have been declared a bastard as well. This might then be grounds enough to say the whole "House of Plantagenet" had no true basis to claim that they were legal descendants of the Merovingians nor would they have a legitimate claim of having their ancestry include the bloodline of Counts of Anjou or Kings of Jerusalem! Again the House of Plantagenet was able to claim ancestral lands that they had no lawful right to.

In *History of the Kings & Queens of England* by David Williamson, the groupings of the various rulers of England does not classify Henry II as a Plantagenet king. Instead he is shown as an Angevin king (of Anjou).

However, Henry II still used his father's name of Plantagenet. Henry was born in Le Mans, France in 1113. He was born under Salic Law. His mother was "widowed." Again, under English Law, a king could not marry a widow. When I went back to Henry I's lineage, I found to my surprise, Henry I's father was known as William I, or William the Conqueror or William the Bastard![5]

In my research, I learned that the Angevin symbol was a sprig of broom, or genus *planta genista*, which gave the House of Plantagenet its name. That title might date back to Henry II in 1154. It was not used by the English royal family of the fifteenth century. To call the Kings of England from 1272 to 1399 Plantagenet is a fiction. There is some justification for treating the rulers from Edward I to Richard II as a distinct group.[6]

In a copy of *The Knights of the Garter, 1348–1939*, by Edmund H. Fellowes (1939), it shows the names of people registered in that order as far back as 1348. Richard III was registered there as a member of the Plantagenet family. He was shown to have been registered in that same volume in 1465. Plantagenet members were registered there as late as 1842. In this same publication, many people, mostly men, were registered in the roll of the Knights of the Garter. However, there is a section at the end where women were registered and today women of royalty are registered in this order. Now, I want to explain how registration in the Order of the Garter was applied and who would take part in building this "New Empire" and what parts they would all play.[7]

Membership in such private groups, such as the Order of the Garter, drew in some very powerful heads of state from all over Europe. This helped to give Edward IV's government an international flair. The new name for a new identity he used, even for members of his own widespread family, was "Plantagenet," to make them feel royal and very important. Well, it seemed to work for him and his government. Edward's IV's ancestor, Edward III, had founded the Order of the Garter in England in 1348. Edward IV wanted to rebuild the Order.

Historians may have a tendency to want to look at this as a "make-believe empire." This is not a portion of English history for me to judge. That is not my intent here. My main concern and interest is what Edward was trying to accomplish with the group surrounding him.

Geoffrey Plantagenet, of the line of the Counts of Anjou, was the father of Henry II. When Edward IV took on the Plantagenet family name, that name supposedly went all the way back to the year 1151. The odd thing about this part of history involving the War of the Roses is that, although the Yorkist and the Lancastrian families seemed to be fighting each other as distinct groups, I discovered that the Plantagenet name was used by both families.

When young Edward was old enough to understand, Jane de Wigmore told him a story. She said, "My husband, Owain Ryes-Jones, was killed in March of 1461, at the same time as your mom Eleanor's husband, Sir Thomas Butler. Also, Sir John Grey, who was married to Elizabeth Woodville, was killed in the Battle of St. Albans in 1461 as well. These men were all loyal Lancastrain knights. Edward then married Elizabeth in 1464, while he was still married to your mom. When Edward got back to Sudeley Castle after waging war with his Yorkist army in February 1462, he found out about Lady Eleanor and Lady

Jane exchanging babies with each other. He had won a major victory against the Lancasterian army and had gone to London to be crowned as King of England."

I now understood why Jane was telling young Edward the things she was telling him. She was trying to give him some idea of his personal history up to that time. At first I found this piece kind of boring but now I find it, like many other pieces I have found in this whole story, was another jewel for me.

I could not have made this all up. When I went to do the research I found that two of the men were killed in battle in the same year, 1461. These two men were husbands of two women that Edward would marry, and the third man, Owain Rhys-Jones, was the husband of Jane de Wigmore, who was mentioned in the dreams. Was this a coincidence or part of a well laid plan? I don't know, but I find it a very strange occurrence considering the outcome. I had not suspected this kind of behavior from Edward during the time I've studied him but I didn't know if he was capable of these kind of tactics on the battlefield. I believe this sort of thing did happen on the battlefield, more than we may be aware of. This tactic would work a lot better than perhaps being accused of murder and in the way it happened there would be no investigations.

In August of 1473, Elizabeth had a son at the Dominican Friary in Shrewsbury.[8] The fact that Edward and Elizabeth would have had a child in Shrewsbury, I found very strange, given the fact that Shrewsbury was an ancient stronghold of the Talbot family. This was Lady Eleanor's family and they were known traditionally to be staunch Lancastrians in that area and are still there today.

CHAPTER FIFTEEN
Edward IV: The Unlikely Marriages

During the period from 1461 to 1464, Edward IV was concentrating on two main parts of his kingship. First, he wanted to marry a woman with which to have his children. Edward was known to be tall and good looking and it was commonly known that he was quite a ladies' man. Many historians believed he could have had any woman of royalty that he may have fancied. There were some rumours around that Edward might marry Katherine, the niece of Duke Philip of Burgundy.

However, Edward had his own marriage plans. Much to the amazement of his court, in 1461, in what they called at that time a precontract ceremony, he married Lady Eleanor Butler née Talbot, a woman of good royal status. Then, in 1464, again to everyone's amazement, Edward married Elizabeth Woodville, while he was still married to Lady Eleanor.[1]

Upon learning of this marriage, I asked myself, *What was Edward thinking when he did this or was he thinking at all?* Then again, *What was Eleanor thinking or even still, did she have a choice in the matter?* As I started studying this situation more closely, I began to see what I thought had taken place. I still didn't have a clear idea as to what prompted Edward's final decision to marry these two women. That is still an historical mystery even today. Why did these supposed marriages become so mysterious? Why did so many people try to obliterate Eleanor's image and name from English history? Edward IV was not an intellectual himself but he knew how to use people to get what he wanted. Many who knew him considered him to be a good business-man and a shrewd politician.

Clarence was the middle brother between Edward and Richard. He wanted to be king. When he found out Edward had married Elizabeth Woodville he saw there might be a chance for him to unseat Edward. He began claiming Edward's marriage to Elizabeth was null and void because English tradition did not allow kings to marry widows.[2]

Edward had married Elizabeth Woodville in 1464 but their two sons and daughter were declared bastards later on, because Edward was already married to Lady Eleanor Talbot-Butler in what was known as a precontract marriage agreement. Historians have stated over and over that this marriage between Edward and Eleanor was not a legal marriage. Now I have discovered that it has been stated that Edward IV and Elizabeth lived together for nineteen years and were never married because their ceremony wasn't considered legal. However, historian David Williamson has said: "On May 1st, 1464, Edward was married in a somewhat furtive manner at the parish church of Grafton Regis, Northhamptonshire. His bride was Elizabeth, a lady some five years his senior and the widow of Sir John Grey, who was killed at the second battle of St. Albans in 1461."[3] In my opinion, this statement doesn't say a priest was present, which would have made the marriage legal.[4]

At this point in the writing this manuscript I want to say I have been appalled by reading a whole volume on the life of Edward IV and finding no mention of Lady Eleanor Talbot-Butler; not one word! That has become one of my main efforts of concern in wanting to write this book. She has repeatedly been written right out of the history of England.

Lady Eleanor was married to Sir Thomas Butler in 1450. They were both from prominent Irish families. They didn't have any children. Sir Thomas Butler was killed in support of the Lancastrian cause in March of 1460. They were together for 11 years and seemed to get along well.

This was one of the points at which I seemed to look at Edward as not such a good fellow. I thought at first Edward could have had Sir Thomas singled out and killed on the battlefield, so he could take control of Eleanor and her properties. The main thing I found wrong with that theory was that Edward's whole family and Edward himself were certainly not wanting for more property or wealth; they had plenty. So, I still couldn't see why Edward wanted to be with Eleanor so much. I really don't see him as being so full of love or being a person of long enduring relationships. In my opinion, he didn't marry for love he married for purpose!

I believe now very strongly that in the end, Edward wanted to antagonize the Talbot family, which had a long history of involvement in Lancastrian politics. Now I believe he put Eleanor under "house arrest," for hiding her baby boy so he couldn't have him killed. He was also outsmarted by Jane de Wigmore and her clan in the process. That is another reason why I believe he had gone to de Wigmore Castle, and tried to destroy as much of it possible could before he left to go to London to be crowned as king. He did not want other troops to use it to fight him from either.

On the other side, I couldn't understand why Eleanor would be so willing to start a new relationship with Edward. Edward was a man who some said had many romantic encounters with many of the women of his time. Eleanor, I believe, must certainly not have been looking for an amorous encounter so soon after losing the man she had just spent the last ten plus years with. She may even have suspected Edward had something to do with her husband being singled out and killed on the battlefield.

It was said in the history that, in about 1450, Eleanor had married Sir Thomas Butler, then they both went to Sudeley Castle to live. Sir Thomas was killed in battle in March 1460. Lord Sudeley had given Sudeley Castle and two manor houses in Warwickshire to the couple upon their marriage, but he failed to get the King's license beforehand. Edward now confiscated these properties. Eleanor went to see Edward and asked him for the return of those same properties, which Edward supposedly granted her in 1461. This history says Edward gave the manor houses back to her but does not say anything about Sudeley Castle, where Lady Eleanor and Sir Thomas had lived for ten years. I would assume Lady Eleanor would have inherited Sudeley Castle when her husband was killed.

Real estate records which I obtained from England show the chain of ownership of the estate of Sudeley Castle as far back as 1066. As it shows in that document it had always been in the Boteler/Butler family since then. In 1469 the record shows: "castle and manor sold or forfeited to Edward IV."[5] Then the record shows: "manor granted to a succession of court favorites." Then in 1469, the record shows: "Sudeley Castle was given to Richard, Edward's brother." Neither Sir Thomas' nor Eleanor's name ever appeared on the long and old real estate record of past owners of Sudeley Castle. Instead, Edward's name appears where Thomas and Eleanor's names should have appeared. Then the next owner of Sudeley was shown as: "Richard, Duke of Glouchester, Edward's brother." You can see this real estate record of Sudeley Castle at the end of this publication.

Then, in my research, I discovered another bit of information about the history of Sudeley Castle. In 1441, Ralph Boteler was created Baron Sudeley. He set about building his castle of stone. In 1461, Edward IV had the Lancastrian Boteler arrested for treason and confiscated his grand home.[6]

I am still plagued with the idea of maybe Lady Eleanor was forced to marry Edward IV. If this in fact had happened, then Eleanor would have known Edward was going to punish her in some way for being of the Talbot family. To me, that was a given. The men of her family were known as the Lords of Shrewsbury, a very powerful Lancastrian family. She was Anglo-Irish and of Catholic birth. She definitely wanted some idea of a family because at this point in her life, she was alone.

She had lost her father Sir John Talbott, 1st Earl of Shrewsbury, he was supporting Henry VI fighting in France in 1453. Then, she lost her brother Sir John Talbott, 2nd Earl of Shrewsbury in a battle in Northampton in 1460, again supporting Henry VI. Finally, she lost her husband in battle. Sir Thomas Boteler was killed in 1460. She had lost her father-in-law, Ralph Sudeley that same year as he was arrested supposedly on charges of treason and taken away. Eleanor never saw him again.[7]

I know that by the time this all happened in her life, Eleanor knew she had nowhere else to turn. All the people in her immediate family were gone. I reasoned that, even if she had to live out the rest of her life under house arrest with Edward, at least it was a roof over her head. She still considered Sudeley Castle her home. She had already taken action to get her son young Edward de Wigmore out of harms way, by getting him to Jane de Wigmore in time for him to survive.

That is how and when I believe Edward placed her under house arrest and held her in the northwest tower of Sudeley Castle. She had received secret messages from Jane while she was incarcerated at Sudeley. She was well aware that her only son had made it to a safe place with good people. That is why she told Jane to have him brought to Sudeley to see her before she passed away.

Another reason why I think Eleanor went to live with Edward and had birthed her son with him is she may have thought there was a slight chance she could unseat Edward from his kingship someday, by getting her son into the kingship.[8] Then, when young Edward had become of age, even if she had to hide him out for a time, she could have at least had some place to live. Sudeley Castle was familiar to her. Also, there may have been a slight chance she would be able to persuade Edward to give her Sudeley Castle back before she died and she could have passed it on to young Edward. I also know from my research that Edward had probably had his eye on Eleanor for quite some time. I believe they even knew each other as children and their families were intertwined. It seems they could have been cousins by marriage, when Eleanor's father remarried.

Then I found references that inferred that Edward himself as King was a bastard. Even Edward and Richard knew that their own brother, Clarence, was spreading rumours about not only Edward being a bastard but both of his sons and a daughter by Elizabeth could be bastards because he had married a widow, Elizabeth Woodville. In England then it was against the law for a king to marry a widow. That would make the marriage illegal also.[9]

Certainly, Eleanor was aware of these allegations herself and she knew her son then could be declared a bastard as well because she was also a widow. But the Church of England never challenged her marriage to Edward. If her marriage to Edward was considered legal, she still had a chance to put her son on the throne. I believe

Edward knew this and that is why he had her well hidden away in Sudeley Castle.

I believe now she stayed at Sudeley Castle under house arrest for a short time and then Edward had her taken to one of the manor houses to live. He treated her well, but she was always under armed guard. Edward could have used this tactic in two ways though. First, it made it look like he had given her property back to her, which the history claimed he did. Secondly, he could have been using her for bait to bring Jane de Wigmore with young Edward to visit with her.

The reason I believe the above is because I could not believe a human being could survive for more than a year under the conditions young Edward first experienced her living in when he had contact with her in 1468 at Sudeley Castle.

I kept going back to that scene where young Edward saw her for the first time and he could not see how she could have lived for at least seven years under those conditions. Now what I think happened was Edward did show compassion to Eleanor and had always had strong feelings for her. Then, Edward did not want to be at Sudeley anymore and he gave the place to his brother, Richard, in about 1467.

When Richard took over Sudeley Castle, he had Eleanor moved back to the castle, as the two manor houses were about to be sold. I believe now that it was Richard who put Lady Eleanor in chains and she had been there for about a year when young Edward first saw her in 1468. In the dreams, young Edward had seen a young man of about 15 years old with an older man at Sudeley. I was able to finally identify them from the history as Richard, Duke of Gloucester and his trainer, Sir James Tyrrell. In the dreams I had, Lady Eleanor died in June of 1468 and was buried in the garden below the dungeon tower, the only garden Eleanor could see from where she was being held. I believe if she did in fact marry Edward it was because she had a plan but she ended up sacrificing herself for her whole family and especially her son, Edward de Wigmore.

Edward IV was an attractive young man and could have married some of the most wealthy women in Europe. Marriage with him could have been a great political asset. Richard Neville, who was his chief counselor, urged a marriage alliance with France.

Elizabeth Woodville was described in most accounts as being of lowly origins. The Woodvilles were of Norman descent. They were an old family of minor gentry who settled in Northamptonshire during the reign of Henry II in France. They were given lands in that country and knighthood and were on the Council of Henry VI. Their son, Richard was born in 1405 and was knighted by Henry in 1426. In 1436, Sir Richard married Princess Jacquetta of Luxembourg, a widow of Henry V's brother, the Duke of Bedford. She was the daughter of the French Count of St. Pol and a descendant of Charlemagne.

The family's loyalties had always been to the House of Lancaster. Elizabeth, the oldest daughter married a Lancastrian knight, Sir John Grey of Gorby, and went to live on his estate in Leicestershire. When the War of the Roses started, Sir John was killed at the Battle of St. Albans in March 1461.

In the spring of 1464, Edward was going to another clash with Henry VI. On the way, he went to Lord River's manor at Grafton Regis. Here, on 1 May, Edward IV married Elizabeth Woodville. There was no indication of there being a priest or witnesses according to Williamson.[10]

After having worked with the research for this manuscript for as long as I have now, I have just realized that there is something seriously wrong with some of the recorded dates I had built into this story.

For instance, in the dreams, as in the history books, Lady Eleanor had her home Sudeley taken from her by Edward IV shortly after her husband Sir Thomas Butler had been killed in early 1460. When Eleanor went to petition Edward in early 1461, as the research shows, to get the castle back, Edward had asked Eleanor to marry him. Whether she said yes or no doesn't matter, she ended up living there again anyway. In the dreams, Eleanor became pregnant and in late 1461, a male child was born. This male child is registered in all the research I have read as being born in early 1467–68. Shortly after that it shows Eleanor died with her male child in infancy in 1468 as well.[11] In my dream, this male child was already born by the time Edward came back to Sudeley Castle in January 1461.

When Edward IV returned to Sudeley, he was told by one of the house keepers that Eleanor had given birth to a male child. By that time, Jane de Wigmore had taken Eleanor's son and exchanged her male child who had died in infancy. Eleanor did that because she knew Edward would have their son killed so he couldn't be a contender for kingship. In late January, Edward stormed off to go find that new son of his. Jane de Wigmore and her family were gone and had hidden his new son away.[12] The history books record, in February 1461 Edward won a decisive victory from de Wigmore Castle and went to London to be crowned.

Finally, if young Edward had been born in late 1461 he still would have been seven or almost eight years old, if he had seen his mother in my dreams in 1468. He always wanted to act older in the dreams than he really was. He could barely understand what was going on when he went to see his mother for the first and last time.

Another issue here is Edward had married Elizabeth Woodville in 1464 which it is stated in all the history I have read on Edward IV. Then the records show Lady Eleanor had gone to see Edward in 1461 after her husband was killed to try to get her properties back from him. That is when it was recorded that Edward proposed marriage to Lady Eleanor. Then they were supposedly married in a precontract marriage agreement in 1461. The history records all show Lady Eleanor Talbot gave birth to a son in 1467–68. The male child died in infancy and Lady Eleanor died that same year as well. If this were true, that meant Edward was married to Elizabeth Woodville when Lady Eleanor had her son in 1468.

The history says Lady Eleanor died in 1468 and Edward married Elizabeth Woodville in 1464. The only problem there is young Edward would have only been just three or four years old when he went to see his mother, Lady Eleanor, for the first and last time. In my dreams, the young son of Edward and Eleanor was very young but he wasn't three or even four years old when he saw his birth mother just before she died in late 1468. He would have been too young to ride a horse alone all the distance he had to ride to Lorne's farm and back to go see his mother.

Again, I can't possibly see how Eleanor could have lived under house arrest for seven or eight years under the squalid conditions she had to exist in. I don't see how she could have lived even one year under those conditions. One record stated she went to stay at a Carmelite mission in Norwich in June of 1468. In answer to a letter I sent them I found out they had no record of her ever being there or having an infant born and die there.[13]

In conclusion, if Eleanor was already dead by 1464 and her male child was assumed dead, then Edward's way was legally clear to marry Elizabeth Woodville and perhaps his children would not have been judged to be bastards. They would have been totally free to become kings if they desired. I believe that was what Edward had planned. Correct dates are very important in documenting history, but sometimes they get confused, sometimes by mistake and sometimes on purpose. I can see how the dates could have been wrong in my dreams, but the dates in this case seem very confused and could be wrong as well.

In the written history Edward's marriages did cause divisions in the royal family. The King's own mother, the Duchess of York, said that Edward was conceived in adultery, and couldn't become king. Both the King's younger brothers, the Duke of Clarence and Richard, Duke of Gloucester were not pleased at all. Clarence was next in line to be king. Richard, being better at concealing his thoughts, remained calm.

From the research I had been studying, I began to see what seemed to be a pattern that Edward was creating whether willfully or by mistake. There was turmoil within his own family as well the whole of the Yorkist dynasty. After all the details I had considered about Edward's political life and then he went and purposely married two women, whose families were avid supporters of the House of Lancaster.

This was the dynasty he had spent most of his active military carreer fighting and then his own daughter married Henry VII, again from the House of Lancaster. King Richard was killed on the battlefield by his brother-in-law, Henry VII, and his Lancastrian army.

Edward had purposely taken wealth and properties from Lancastrian nobles and give to his large Woodville family, who also had serious Lancastrian roots. He got them registered in the Order of the Garter and built his own new little empire. In the end his own nobles who had trusted him lost faith in him. I didn't have any idea why a king of his supposed political awareness would follow the path he did. I could see that Edward didn't appoint people to high positions in his government who were really aware of how to run a government, except some of his old faithful nobles.

I started looking at some of the areas that I could see as possible weaknesses in Edward's maneuvering but then I realized I am not a politician. Throughout this manuscript, I was just going by plain common sense and my intuition to see if I could come through with my own reasons for events I was trying to make sense of.

Soon, I found myself grounded out and very confused by this convoluted piece of history I was trying to work with. I came to a point once again where I was almost ready to say all of this was a waste of time and way over my head. I felt I just wasn't getting anywhere! The history I was finding was seemingly going in circles.

When Edward's brother Clarence was put to death, the way was then clear for his young son to carry the kingship. His brother, Duke of Gloucester, who had been faithful to him in his reign, would just have to wait a little longer for his turn to be king. In the dreams, Edward still hadn't found young Edward de Wigmore but he hadn't given up on finding him someday. Suddenly, Edward, passed away at age 41.

Now young Edward still being alive mattered more to Richard as he became king in 1483. Edward de Wigmore would have been about 23 years old at this time in my dreams. Then Richard III was killed at the Battle of Bosworth Field by Lancastrian troops. When Henry VII finally became king, he couldn't feel secure until that document, *Titulus Regius*, was destroyed. Even though Lady Eleanor had perhaps already been dead since 1464, Henry still ordered all the copies of that famous document to be surrendered and destroyed because Lady Eleanor Talbot-Butler's name was still in there to haunt him. He knew very well he did not want it talked about for one reason among many. He may have known young Edward de Wigmore was still alive at 25 years old out there somewhere. He was now the perfect age to challenge his kingship and could have possibly done so at any time.

King Henry knew a lot about young Edward de Wigmore, because his wife was King Edward's daughter Elizabeth, who wasn't exactly on real firm footing herself, because of allegations that she was a bastard.

She would have kept Henry closely informed as to young Edward's whereabouts if need be. Henry had a lot more to be concerned about, because he wasn't on firm ground when it came to his line of succession to the kingship. He could have had young Edward de Wigmore dealt with in short order if he had tried for the kingship.

CHAPTER SIXTEEN
Edward IV: Rebuilding The Order Of The Garter

E dward's first reign had only lasted for nine years, from 1461 to 1470 when he was run out of England by Henry VI's army and had to go back into France and regroup. He got a break when Henry was killed in battle. He became king once again and started his new rule in 1471 and ruled England until he died suddenly in 1483.

When Edward went back for his second rule, he still had the framework for his old empire. Some of the historians who watched Edward's rule very closely could see that he was more organized than most critics gave him credit for. In my research, I was starting to see an evolving pattern in his rule and his personality.

As I have already stated, Edward had already found the women he thought he needed. He had quietly married a not-so-royal woman by the name of Elizabeth Woodville. The only problem was he was already married to a woman named Lady Eleanor Talbot-Butler and now he was ready to work on the rebuilding of the Order of the Garter. I hadn't yet come to the reason for this Order of the Garter, which was implemented during the reign of his ancestor Edward III. Secondly, I still wasn't any closer to the reasons why Edward IV would want to re-build that Order, especially in a form of such grandeur. As I followed further along considering this theme, I found some of his reasoning becoming apparent.

I perceived Edward would use appointments in the Order as bait to world leaders in order to build a worldwide commercial network, the like of which had not been known in England up until then. This was an idea and dream of Edward's ancestor, Edward III. Using the same basic model, Edward was determined to make the Order a part of his own dream and this is where he would shine as a world leader.

In the study of Edward IV rebuilding the Order of the Garter, I found this chapter of my manuscript very set apart from the other chapters. I didn't know why that was. I remembered going to my favorite used book store, and how I was finding a lot of second hand books by famous English historians. One day after I was getting on with this research, I found this thin little volume in that same store and the title was *The Knights of the Garter, 1348–1939*. I was so proud of myself. I had paid dearly for it but I couldn't wait to read it and find out what it had to offer.[1]

This book was edited by a gentleman named Edmund H. Fellowes. He was known as a minor canon of Windsor and an Honorable Fellow of Oriel College, Oxford. Later I had found out that this Mr. Fellowes was very close to the royal family and his son married Lady Diana's sister.

Mr. Fellowes Sr. had worked on this book with the help of the Canons and Minor Canons at St. George's Chapel, Windsor Castle in 1937 to 1939. That book became one of my most prized history books. In just 115 pages, I had a record of names that spanned over 500 years of English history. One thing that enamored me to this book was that the name of one of my ancestors, William Paget, was listed there because he had been a privy councilor to Henry VIII and Henry had him admitted to the Order in 1547, as Sir William Paget, 1st Lord Paget de Beaudesert.[2]

In my research I found the Order had been originally organized in 1348. In the volume I had found, there were a number of prominent men during the reign of Edward III that helped found the Order of the Garter. There was too much involved with an effort such as this to have been completed by a few persons.

Edward III was in the kingship of England for fifty years. It became evident that his reign was definitely a time of great success for the merchant class of England. At that time there were only twenty-four knights allowed as members at any one time.[3]

Edward IV, as historians have commented, used membership in the Garter as a diplomatic weapon or tool. There were many foreign heads of state registered in the Garter rolls in Edward's time as well as today. I was very surprised to see how far and wide they ranged throughout my copy of that publication.

If Edward needed to impress a certain person of importance to him, he would readily have their name registered in the Garter, complete with all the side benefits that may have accompanied that person's registration.

Among the state dignitaries registered were: Ferdinand I, King of Naples; Francisco Sforza, Duke of Milan; Duke Charles of Burgundy; King Ferdinand of Castile and Aragon; and John II, King of Portugal. They also included Federigo da Montefeltro, Duke of Urbino, commander of the papal troops, elected in 1474. His influence at Rome helped to procure from Sixtus IV, a "grant of indulgences and remission of sins," to all visitors to the Garter chapel at Windsor in October 1476. Election to the Order remained much up to Edward's personal discretion. Admission to this "charmed circle" had no set criterion. If Edward wanted a certain person admitted, then it was so.[4]

At Windsor Castle, the building of a new Chapel of St. George's was a symbol of Edward's love of splendid architecture. This was Edward's supreme achievement as a patron. The building of the new chapel was intended as a monument to the House of York and Edward intended it as a resting place for his own bones; and it is today.

In April 1483, Edward IV became ill and, as it was noted, lingered for about nine days before dying. This sudden illness took him and his family and friends by surprise because he had been active and was not a sickly person. Some historians said he had taken on a lot of weight in recent years from overindulging in food. He spent his last days trying to set things right in his government as well as his family. He reportedly died on 9 April 1483. Right away the whisperings and the gossip started and speculation as to who would became the next king or queen was heating up.

In 1482, John II of Portugal was installed in the Order of the Garter, but something happened and then the record states he was not installed until his re-election in 1488 when he was officially installed in the Order.

Anthony Woodville, (Earl Rivers) the son of Elizabeth, had always liked to travel amongst the Royalty of Portugal, Spain and Italy. I think Anthony tried to get the King of Portugal installed in the Garter but Edward had too many other problems to keep him busy at that time.

Richard was watching this and knew from the history that other Kings of Portugal had been installed in the Garter years before. In 1435, Edward, King of Portugal, son of Philippa, sister of Henry IV, King of England, was installed.

The historical resources I have read seemed to note Richard had been monitoring the actions of the Woodville family very closely since Edward had married Elizabeth. Suddenly when Edward died, one of Richard's first moves toward becoming King Richard III was to interrupt Anthony Woodville's friendship with the King of Portugal from using the Garter to make political inroads for his family, as his mother Elizabeth, made her way to become the new Queen of England. Their family had tasted political power and liked the taste.[5]

It was then I began to realize, that Richard desperately wanted to be king. With this in mind, Richard knew the time to move had come; he had to take control. He was well aware that the Woodville family, in their time under Edward's wing, had amassed great wealth and strength in numbers. I believed they thought, as a united family, they had a good chance to put Elizabeth on the throne and be rid of Richard and the House of York, for good! They had two distinct ways to power they could follow.

They knew as a family they weren't too well liked. Even so Elizabeth Woodville was Edward's wife and was already a Queen and could possibly remain as Queen of the kingdom. She could rule for a few years until Young Edward V came of age and then he could rule. If that plan didn't work they could go on with what Edward wanted them to do in the first place. Elizabeth could become the protector of young King Edward V, as that is what a lot of the people wanted to see happen. Either way they would have been in a good position of political control from behind the scenes.[6]

Richard of Gloucester, knew now he had to seek power quickly and maybe even by force in 1483. When Edward died Richard, even though he was 31 years old and well versed in how to run the government, must have felt frightened and alone.

Richard had to make sure he was the sole protector of Edward V after his father's sudden death. Edward was only 12 years old and his father had already appointed Richard the protector of his nephew as the new king. As many of the historians of the time, such as Dominic Mancini and Sir Thomas More recorded, Richard did manage to be granted the legal protector of King Edward V.

Finally, after Edward IV's burial ceremony, Richard rode with his guards to meet the young king and escort him to London. As it turned out, the young king-to-be was escorted to the Tower of London, later joined with his younger brother, and neither of them were ever heard of or seen again.

Richard did get his chance to become king as Richard III. He was king for some two years, from June of 1483 to August 1485, when he was killed at Bosworth Field, by Henry VII's Lancastrian army.[7]

In my view of world history, I see that historians often times don't stop to ask why world events or even simple, everyday events, happen the way they do. In fact, world politics it seems, are enacted even today, by a type of "round table mentality," such as I have discovered here in researching the Middle Ages. One of the famous Dukes of this period of history, when he found out King Edward's wife Queen Elizabeth might be trying to become Queen of England after his death, had remarked something to the effect that, "Women should not lead kingdoms. That should be left to the barons and nobles that know how to do that sort of thing."

One of the interesting facts I found, in a closer look at the Order of the Garter, was that women were allowed to be installed in the Order. The Netherlands today were once settled by people referred to as the Salic Franks. They developed a group of legal codes and one of these so-called Salic Laws that had developed from these Salic codes, excluded women from the lines of succession to a throne. I found it strange that England, in its rule, did not encourage women to be their leaders, but at the same time, they did not discourage them from leadership and still do not today. An appointment to the Order seems to have been the prerogative of the sovereign alone, but the women had no place in the Chapel stalls and no stall-plates or banners. There is, surprisingly, a list of the names of women who had been installed in the Order of the Garter over a long period of history. I wanted to show that women have played a part in this Order of the Garter across a large span of history just as they do today. The now deceased Margaret Thatcher and many of the royalty of England have been and still are members of the Order of the Garter. After reading this little book, I have concluded that the Order of the Garter seemed to help heal some of the wounds the War of the Roses had caused. It seems also that King Edward IV, having set his government on a new departure, caused England to rise as a world economy, which it has remained since his reign.[8]

CHAPTER SEVENTEEN
The Passing Of Edward IV

Edward IV, in all his time spent with his wife Elizabeth and her family, never allowed them to enjoy the material lavishness that a lot of royalty did in their time. The Woodvilles did not get to experience the patronage in land, wardship and profitable offices which the Neville family and the men like Hastings and others of a select few received in the early years of Edward's reign. The Woodvilles seemed to remain highly unpopular. Dislike of the Woodvilles was prominent in Yorkist politics. Some historians believe that resentment was caused by the whole family's rapid rise to prominence.

Their reputation was said to stem from their own behavior. As a family, the Woodvilles were not known to exhibit a lot of charm or concern for others. Earl Rivers and the Duchess of Bedford seemed to have had a nature marred by greed. They could be overbearing as well.[1]

Anthony Woodville, their oldest son, had literary interests and his early patronage of the painter, Caxton, had gotten him a certain esteem. He traveled widely in Italy, Spain, and Portugal.

The main source of the Woodvilles' unpopularity was the belief that they demanded and expected a lot from the king. When Edward died prematurely in April 1483, no one cared for the idea of the Queen and her family taking over the reins of government, especially Richard.

Westminster Palace was where Edward IV would spend his last Christmas. Some historians at that time believed that he showed signs of not being in his usual form. Some even thought his health seemed to be failing. Even so, surrounded by his family, whom he loved very much, all went well and was marked as a joyful occasion. His court stayed at Westminster Place and made only brief normal visits to Windsor Castle in early 1483. Then, in late March of that year, Edward fell suddenly ill.[2]

As I have already mentioned, Edward died 9 April 1483. There was and still is a lot of speculation as to what may have caused Edward's death. There were so many conflicting views concerning his death that in the end it seemed that serious facts gave way to empty speculation.

An historian of that era, Polydore Vergil was of the opinon that Edward's death was caused from "an unknown disease," but later hinted that the cause could have been poison.[3] Edward Hall, a Tudor chronicler thought Edward could have gotten fever when he was in France and it was worsened by an over indulgence in food. Malaria was still common in Europe in the marshes of the Somme valley.[4] Dominic Mancini, another historian who was following the passing of Edward, had heard in the courts of London that Edward's death had been caused by a serious cold he had gotten on a recent fishing trip. Again, Mancini reported that Edward's love of food had made him heavy and that his sexual extravagance had not decreased over the years.[5] Historian Philippe de Commynes, believed that Edward died of apoplexy (quaterre) brought on by excess.[6]

There was one fact in all the research of what historians had to say about the nature of Edward's illness. Edward didn't die suddenly. It was documented that Edward was still clear enough in his mind to add several changes to his will. Also he tried to reconcile bad feelings among his courtiers. His illness lasted ten days. He became ill on 29 March and he died on Wednesday, 9 April 1483, just short of his forty-first birthday.[7]

The information I studied on the death of Edward left me feeling empty. I didn't feel satisfied with the varied opinions I had researched. Being such experts on King Edward's life, I had expected more from the historians of the day. The end of Edward's life was left in confusion as to the causes of his death.

Edward's kingship was being sought after by the Woodvilles and Richard, just as a start. Why, I thought, was Edward's death surrounded by so much uncertainty? I went back over the information from various historians on Edward's death. I found I couldn't accept most of their conclusions. I got the same let down feeling that there was something missing or just not being told.

From all the information on Edward's passing I had read, I could see no one would commit themselves to a definite cause of death, not the doctors nor the historians nor chroniclers. There seemed to be a whispering undercurrent as to the causes of Edward's death.

Here was a king dead at 41. He was an active person always on the move. He hadn't been a sickly person in his early life. Autopsies had not yet come into the medical realm for being used to prove cause of death. I believe many kings had died of poisoning because no one was willing to go as far as to prove their cause of death.

Politically, that wasn't the thing to do. A person could lose their position or job if they dug too deeply into the cause of death, especially of royalty. It didn't matter what the cause of death was to an average citizen.

Everyone seemed to just put Edward IV's death in a neat little package and just move on. The most common cause of Edward's death listed was his overindulgence. He ate too much, he had too much sex, he was overweight, so it was easily concluded that he died of a stroke. Then with the pomp of the burial ceremony another king would enter the annals of history and soon the people would forget all the rumours that may have been prominent at that time.

I could have accepted those opinions at first but then I remembered that comments on Edward's passing stuck with me. The comment was that Edward's death was reported in York on 6 April and his mass was sung the next day, on 7 April. Edward was documented as dying on 9 April 1483.[8]

It seemed to me they were trying to hurry things along a little too quickly for some reason. I do take into account that dates were sometimes wrong or misquoted especially from historical records that old.

I began to believe there were more political motives involved here than were being talked about or were even still in existence. Not many historians were willing to take a chance and go ahead and speak to the issues and say what they really thought had happened. This then, really gave me a motive to study as many of the references as I could find on this passing of a king at age 41. I studied writers, both past and present on this historical event.

Even though Edward was a big eater and may have been vulnerable to a stroke, I don't believe he died of a stroke. It was recorded that he had lived ten days after falling ill. To me it seems to have been a slow death. Also, if he had died of a stroke, it doesn't seem his mind would have been clear enough to concentrate on the issues he was trying to deal with, as was reported. He was going over his final will and that required mental clarity.

Another avenue of approach that I found was that Edward loved his food and he was also an avid bird hunter, mostly dove and quail. I began to believe he may have been fed his favorite birds at Eastertide, (28–30 March) at Westminster. I began to find out about "birders" who raised all sorts of birds to sell to many well-to-do clients in those days.

One of the sources I started looking at, is a book entitled *A Modern Herbal* by Mrs. M. Grieve, who was English and lived and wrote in England in the turn of the last century. I trust her opinion and have used her book as a reference for many years as I am an herbalist. In her volume she wrote about the poison hemlock; she states: "It is by no means an uncommon plant in this country (UK), found on the hedge banks, in neglected meadows, on waste ground and by the borders of streams in most parts of England. The poisonous property occurs in all parts of the plant, though it is stated to be less strong in the root."

I read on further in Mrs. Grieve's work where she states:

> Larks and quail are said to eat poison hemlock with impunity, but their flesh becomes so impregnated with the poison that they become poisonous as food. Like many other poisonous plants, when cut and dried, p. hemlock, loses much of its poisonous properties which are volatile and easily dissipated. Cooking destroys it. Poisoning has occurred from eating the leaves mistaken for parsley, the roots for parsnips and the seeds mistaken for anise seeds. As a medicine (*Conium maculatum*) p. hemlock, is a sedative and antispasmodic, and in sufficient doses, acts as a paralyzer to the centers of motion. On account of its peculiar sedative action on the motor centers hemlock juice is prescribed as a remedy in cases of undue nervous

motor excitability, such as teething in children, and also for epilepsy.

As an inhalation it is said to relieve cough in bronchitis, whooping cough, asthma, etc. In poisonous doses it produces complete paralysis with loss of speech, the respiratory function is at first depressed and ultimately ceases altogether and death results from asphyxia. The mind remains unaffected to the last.[9]

I really came to life when I read the last statement of Mrs. Grieve I recorded here. I read it over and over. I thought this was just one clue but a good one. "The mind remains unaffected until the last." I then referred back to the statement that historian Charles Ross had mentioned that "Edward IV carried on, still clear enough in his mind to add to his last will, and to settle feuds amongst his courtiers."

That information for me alluded to the fact that the cause of Edward's death could have been, in some way, closely connected to the "Poison Hemlock" plant perhaps being used by his physician for his sickness. Maybe Edward's physician had used too much p. hemlock, for his cold or pneumonia. He could have eaten too many birds that weren't quite cooked enough to render them not poisonous. Lastly, I believe someone could have intentionally poisoned him, that knew his eating habits

Then further, I ran across what historian David Williamson says in his piece about Edward's passing, "He was not quite 41 when he died at Westminster, probably of pneumonia caught on a fishing trip."[10] Sir Winston Churchill suggested that Edward had died from an attack of appendicitis.[11]

One of the strangest parts of all the information I could find in relation to Edward's passing was that there was no mention of or at least a study made on Edward's body organs to determine cause of death when they embalmed him.

Then I found an historical piece of information that mentioned Edward had died on 9 April but was not laid to rest until 17 April. This would seemingly have left enough time to study the body further and still had time to embalm him.

Because there was no such thing as autopsy done in those times, there is room here to speculate about whether Edward did die of natural causes or not. A lot of historians were watching to see what the Woodville family's reaction to Edward's passing would be. The Duke of Gloucester, soon to be known as Richard III, was certainly watching the Queen and her family and they were doing the same with Richard. This was an extremely tense time for the whole nation as well for its leaders. Edward IV was dead and buried and that was it for him.

The War of the Roses had seemed as though it was a series of nagging family feuds with the most prominent families squaring off against each other, seeing who could accumulate the most wealth. The nation's people were tired of it. Now in this extreme time for the whole nation, their leader was dead. Whoever was going to lead next had to know how to lead and get settled in position in a hurry!

Richard had waited a long time for this move. He knew that the Woodvilles' old loyalties were subdued but still very much alive and even more so now with the passing of Edward IV. Richard was already 32 years old now and knew his time to become king was running out. Both the Yorks and the Lancasters knew whatever action, in response to Edward's death and the void his passing had left in the political structure of the nation, must be dealt with swiftly. Richard had watched for years how the Queen's family had amassed wealth and power. He knew they wanted to put the young prince Edward on the throne. There was not much time to spare for mourning Edward's passing. Greed and a yearn for power abounded everywhere!

British historian, David Williamson gives his view of how the transition of the new king did take place by commenting:

> When his father died unexpectedly, the twelve year old Prince Edward was residing at Ludlow, one of his official residences, and on receiving the news that he was now king set out for London, to be met on the way at Stony Stratford by his uncle Richard, Duke of Gloucester, on his way down from York. Richard conducted his nephew to London with every sign of loyalty and they were met outside the city by the Lord Mayor and leading citizens, who

escorted them to the Tower, which it is alleged the young king never left again.[12]

Many historians have written about the legacy of King Edward IV. That legacy has gone through a lot of changes in 500 years. I must admit I found him to be an enigma. He could instantly change his direction and not change his determination to do what he intend to do. To me he seemed to single out men on the battlefield, have them killed and take their property. He spent time with two women who were widows of men that recently died on the battlefield fighting his army. Historical records show that Edward worked at destroying the wealthy Plantagenet families that had become Lancasterians. He must have owned more properties than his father.

Edward and Richard both treated Lady Eleanor worse than an animal, holding her under house arrest in chains for years until she died. She was a prisoner there. That part of the dreams was the hardest part for me to witness but the dreams gave me as close a view of the history I'm writing about here as I could possibly get.

Some of the early Tudor historians and writers, such as Sir Thomas More and Polydore Vergil, were in contact with a wide circle of people that knew and had served Edward. In their opinion, he was a businesslike king, who was peaceful and prosperous. He was considered a popular king but his rule had been firm.[13] Then there came a revisionist period, in the 1800s and later, that saw Edward IV as debauched, cruel, avaricious and lazy, capable of energy and decision only in times of crisis.

Edward had become king when he was only nineteen years old. He served two terms as king. His first rule was from 1461 to 1470 and his second was from 1471 to 1483, a 21 year reign. The Order of the Garter had served him well and gave him the honor of being known as an acute business mind. He, in effect, had set England up with the reputation as being a world trader, much like his ancestor, Edward III had wanted. That influence has been copied by nations all over the world.

Sometimes people do not like to see others' successes and can become jealous of their achievements. Many kings and some queens have been hated because of that nature. Many have brought it on themselves by their arrogance. Some of the records that recorded their deeds are not to be found. Some documents concerning their actions are filled with empty rumours that may have made a good story. The past kings and queens cannot defend themselves now. Even in times when their intentions were well placed, still they could be criticized for what they had done, a lot like ordinary people.

CHAPTER EIGHTEEN
Richard III: His Dreams And Nightmares

In English history, the years 1460 to 1487 were years of political upheaval. Within a period of twenty-five years the crown changed hands at least six times. Violence took at least two kings and maybe three. The kings were, Edward IV, Edward V, Richard III.

Now that Edward IV was dead, Richard began to watch every move Elizabeth made, as she was still Edward's Queen. She was supposedly left in charge of Edward V, to help him become the next king. Now here the history seems to go foggy.

Richard made sure that the courts knew he was to be the new young king's protector and run the government for him until he was of the age to do so. That became a highly debated issue between the Woodvilles and Richard, the two assertive camps. Richard realized that the Queen and her family would aid young Edward to become the next king. Richard could feel himself being quickly phased out of the picture.

Richard tried to hide his dislike and jealousies of the Woodvilles. Edward V was twelve years old when his father Edward IV died. Richard could see the writing on the wall and knew young Edward V was destined to become a puppet dominated by the Woodvilles. Richard also knew that this was a perfect set-up for them. He must have reasoned that the Woodvilles were so unpopular that he believed none of them would ever be accepted to be the next leader of the people of England.

The Woodvilles knew as well, if they could stay behind the scenes and still run the government, things could work out well for them.

They also knew they didn't have a choice—they had to pull off their plan or their lives would be on Richard's to-do list.

Richard thought he was the natural choice to act as regent or protector of young Edward, but he also saw himself as the next king of England. Richard didn't have any animosity toward young Edward V; he was his nephew. Even so Richard knew he had the backing of most of the loyal followers of his deceased brother. They all knew the Woodvilles were trying to gain support for young Edward to, in turn, gain more support for themselves. The military who had been loyal to Edward IV was also loyal to Richard but refused to support the Woodvilles.

In the end, the discord between these two rivals helped Richard seize the throne in June of 1483. This being so, the in-fighting had eventually caused a weakening of the Yorkshire politic and created many new divisions. There were still bad feelings left over from Edward marrying into the Woodvilles, a Lancasterian camp. Richard knew he would be facing lots of problems ahead, but he was just enjoying becoming Richard III. He thought he could deal with his problems later.

The Woodvilles were unpopular especially when they showed their ambitions and quick success. Much of these feelings came from just plain prejudice from the notable increase of influence after Edward's second term in 1471. Dislike of the Woodvilles came about not so much because of material and political gains but how fast they made them.[1]

There were seven marriages, all with regal splendor. Elizabeth's father became treasurer and was created an Earl, and Anthony, their son received a grant of the Isle of Wight. All of these advances took only two years after Edward's marriage to Elizabeth. As a family, the Woodvilles were not modest or overly friendly. Like his daughter, Earl Rivers and his wife the Duchess of Bedford were known to be greedy.[2]

Modern attempts to find any political motive for this marriage are very few. Edward didn't need to marry this widow to assert his independence of Warwick and the Nevilles. Edward could have married any woman he wanted, there was no shortage of brides amongst the higher ranks of the English nobility. Edward's motives for this marriage are only a matter of speculation. Historians of that era and even now have noted that the marriage led to the breakdown of the Yorkist dynasty as a political entity.[3]

Historians have said Elizabeth Woodville was far from suitable as a queen. However, Jacquetta, Elizabeth's mother, belonged to the high nobility of Europe. Her father Pierre, Count of St. Pol, was a powerful French magnate and through him she could claim descent from the Emperor Charlemagne himself. Many historical writers of that period had emphasized that the social status of the family was not as lowly as many historians have assumed.[4]

Right after Edward's passing, his brother now as Richard III was trying to justify his claim to the throne by circulating a story which no one believed at first. He was claiming the sons of Edward IV were bastards, because he was still married to Lady Eleanor Butler née Talbot while he was married to Elizabeth Woodville.

Richard's seizure of power may have involved the judicial murders of young Edward's uncle, Anthony Woodville, Earl Rivers and of the Queen's younger son, Richard Grey; then there was the execution without trial of Edward IV's loyal supporter, Lord Hastings. Hastings could not tolerate the imprisonment of Edward's two young sons. These two sons then mysteriously disappeared from the Tower and where never seen again.

Suddenly, Richard III found himself in one of the great power struggles of his life. Since he was Edward IV's younger brother by ten years, having been born in 1452, he had always stayed fairly well-hidden in the shadow of his brother but had remained extremely loyal to him. Edward IV was, in his own right, from a very early age, an aggressive leader. So Richard was very comfortable following his brother's lead and didn't have to make his own decisions until suddenly Edward became ill and passed away.

I realized now that the young man I saw and heard giving orders to the kitchen staff and walking out with the tall man was, in fact, Richard, Duke of Gloucester, at 16 years old. I have discovered in my research that Richard, at the time I saw him for the first time in my dream, had just been given Sudeley Castle by his big brother, Edward IV. I also figured out who the tall man was with him in that same dream. He was a man named Sir James Tyrrell; he was at that time a military trainer for Richard. According to historian David Williamson in his book *History of the Kings & Queens of England*,

> Sir James Tyrrell later confessed under torture to the killing of the two sons of Edward IV and was beheaded in 1502.[5]

The call for suppression of the document *Titulus Regius* could have affected Henry VII's kingship in serious ways. Tyrrell was killed near the end of Henry's rule which was in 1509. With Tyrrell gone, the King could relax because Tyrrell could now take the blame for many issues. Henry was more worried about preening his son, Henry VIII for the throne than his own kingship, which only lasted another seven years.

From the above information, I thought maybe Tyrrell knew too much about Edward's marriages to two different women at the same time. He also possessed first hand knowledge of the happenings during the reign of Edward IV. He must have known what happened to the two Princes and the secrets of the vying for the kingship of Richard III and what transpired during the *Act of Settlement* period.

In the dreams, I had at least learned that both Richard III and James Tyrrell were party to Lady Eleanor's incarceration. They did nothing to ameliorate her living conditions near the end of her life. They both witnessed her starvation and death. Richard became responsible for her immediate burial. She was buried in a nondescript grave next to Jane de Wigmore's infant son, Larson, in the garden under the dungeon tower.

I learned that Richard was the new owner and full time occupant of Sudeley Castle when Lady Eleanor died there. This fact was proven by a real estate record I got from the UK showing all the previous owners of that estate.[6]

After Edward had died and Richard had taken the throne, some historians and chroniclers seemed to focus on issues of what they labeled as Richard's cynicism and ruthlessness. They believed those traits had cost him the support of many of the leading gentry of southern and western England. Many of these people were former servants of King Edward IV. They had close personal associations with his court and were loyal to the true Yorkist line.

About three months after Richard took the throne, dangerous movements were starting to happen in the southern counties. These former supporters of the Yorkists cause were calling for the release of the princes from the Tower. Rumours began spreading that the sons of Edward IV were already dead, many speculating that Richard had them killed. Now the rumours were becoming widely believed. The resentment and suspicion held by the southern gentry led to a scheme to depose him in favor of the unknown Henry Tudor, who would become Henry VII. He was to marry Edward's eldest daughter, Elizabeth of York, who earlier had been labeled a bastard, along with her two brothers, by their uncle Richard, Duke of Gloucester.

I found in my copy of *The Knights of the Garter, 1348–1939* a listing for Edward's two sons. It states,

> 1475 (214) Edward (Plantagenet) Prince of Wales. Afterwards Edward V, King of England. Murdered with his brother Richard, Duke of York, in the Tower of London.[7]

I believe this does show that the Knights of the Garter of this era knew that the two sons of Edward IV were in fact murdered. This seemed to be common knowledge among that group of people at that time. If anyone would have full knowledge of the goings on of the nation, I believe the Knights of the Garter would know for sure.

Richard, soon to be Richard III, was now in something of a dilemma. Many people were not enamoured with Richard at this point. He had many problems he was now having to deal with. I did think that he could have easily been completely set up, in a well thought out scheme, to take the fall for the death of his brothers, Clarence and Edward and Edward's two sons, Edward and Richard. With four key members of the same family being kings and potential kings, now all were assumed dead and out of the way, this had cleared the way for both Richard and the Woodvilles, to each seek the throne of England.

Richard's short reign lasted only two years, from 1483 to 1485. In a summary of that reign Richard was not dealt with kindly. He is said to have destroyed his own Yorkist dynasty. That dynasty's strife stands in contrast to the solidarity of the Lancasterian dynasty in that same era. The controversy of Richard's kingship is still present in English history today but there is a very strong revivalist movement to clear the name of Richard III.

The Woodvilles would have had a clear path to declare, and totally change over to, their old Lancastrian lines. They easily could have become more wealthy than they had already become. I was slowly becoming an apologist for Richard but I still thought he was self-centered and greedy. I thought he would have gotten rid of anyone who might try to oppose his move to assume what he thought was his rightful position as King of England. That had been his dream since he was a child; now he was in his early 30s. He knew that this would be the fulfillment of his lifelong dream. Richard realized this was it. He had to make his move for kingship now or the chance could be gone. He did not know this was the beginning of his worst nightmare.

Richard found himself in a dilemma, when he did realize that one of his most loyal supporters, in the person of Henry Stafford, known as the Duke of Buckingham was plotting to help bring Henry Tudor (later Henry VII), to the throne. As luck would have it, this secret rebellion against Richard didn't come off so well from the start. It seems the weather was bad with lots of rain. Buckingham's Welsh troops deserted him and his hiding place was revealed to Richard's loyal supporters. He was brought to Salisbury and executed in 1483. This totally weakened the sense of rebellion against Richard III.

One writer who wrote about Richard III was Sir Thomas More who was born in England in 1478. Richard was killed in battle in 1483. More wrote his work on Richard when he was about 20 years old, by about 1513, but didn't publish any of it until 1557. When you do the math, Richard had been gone for 74 years by then. Not quite a lifetime but long enough to let the public rumours about him cool down and become known as fact.

William Shakespeare was born in 1564. He published his *Richard III*, in 1592, 35 years after More published his final work on Richard and 109 years after Richard had died. Again, so much time had passed, that Shakespeare could say whatever he wanted to about Richard's lifetime. There weren't many critics that knew much first hand information about Richard III still alive to say he was wrong or right. He painted Richard as a "deformed monster." The shock effect worked because the play became very popular, but it may not have been very historically correct. Richard III is still a very popular play, even today.

Shakespeare, in his play *Richard III*, never mentioned Lady Eleanor Talbot-Butler.[8] He must have been aware of her at least from his friend Sir Thomas More. He must have known about young Edward de Wigmore, the only son of Lady Eleanor, who was said to have been born in 1467–68 and lived to be 76 years old, which meant Edward would have died in 1544.

One of the areas I had covered over and over was whether or not, Edward IV and Lady Eleanor Butler had really been legally married in a "precontract ceremony." I couldn't understand why Richard III wanted to keep that issue alive. To me that proved the marriage was legal or how else could Richard have used that to prove Edward's sons and daughter were bastards.

As I went on with this project, it became clear to me what the Yorkists, with Richard now their king, were really after and what their next moves might be.

Richard was declared King in 1483, with the death of his brother Edward IV. In his first and only Parliament in 1484, what was referred to as the *Act of Settlement* or finally, *Titulus Regius*, was committed to English history.

As the historian David Williamson wrote:

> The two armies met at Bosworth Field on 22 August 1485. The king's army was twice the size of Henry's, but the turning point of the battle came when Lord Stanley, Henry's stepfather, and his 7,000 man army deserted Richard and went over to Henry. Richard fought bravely to the last but was finally cut down.

CHAPTER NINETEEN
Lady Eleanor And The Three Kings

I didn't realize when I first started having these dreams and then began writing this manuscript that the history would involve three consecutive kings' reigns. The historians I began to read and study concerning this time frame all seemed to have been unwavering in their own individual views and opinions of how they perceived the history of that era. That is only to be expected, but this particular part of English history seemed to take a turn and evolved into a convoluted medium which was no longer logical to me. There was a type of screening of the facts that I hadn't experienced in the research I had already done.

However, as my studies of the research became more refined, the truth seemed to have been put away for future historians to explore and draw their own conclusions. Many of the conclusions I studied seemed to end in question marks.

I have experienced this situation in trying to finalize this manuscript and bring my conclusions together, and finally I have given this "political sleight of hand" a name: *purposeful delusion.* This is a method monarchies and governments have used for centuries to delude the general public since the printing press was invented. Governments all over the world have used this method to confuse the issues when need be to excuse leaders of their shortcomings.

Much of the chronicled writings of this era were lost, burned or somehow misplaced. So for historians to be able to write a balanced view of this history remains a chore and almost an impossibility. With very few solid facts available from this period of history, how can there be any writings about this era that are not based on sheer speculation? At least I had my dreams to help guide me through the research. At times I have seen my dreams as a more reliable source of information than the so-called real history.

This was also the era of the War of the Roses. However, that war from my view was just an isolated struggle between two of the wealthiest dynasties of this era, the Yorks and the Lancasters. The dynasty that was in control of the throne at the time would take the wealth from the other dynasty and disburse it to their loyal supporters. It is an historical fact that in the thirty years of this so-called war, there was a little over three months of live combat. Supposedly, only seven of the old aristocratic families became extinct during the War of the Roses.[1]

When I finally did delve into this part of English history, the reasons why I didn't want to study this history became evident all over again. My natural dislike of this history was instinctual. Over the years I have learned to trust my instincts and this time I was right once again.

In putting this manuscript together I have had to read volume upon volume of some of the most boring writing I have ever read. I was a slow reader in school but I knew I had to do this reading to try to fit my four dreams into the written history of the era I'm writing about.

When I did find that the subject matter of my dreams was a part of the existing English history, I felt I had it made. It didn't take me long though to figure out that this was going to be a much larger chore than I thought.

I began to read older historians who had spent their whole lives writing what they thought was the truth. Then, I began reading the more contemporary historians' works. I found a lot more history that had been written poorly because many of the writers had fallen into the same traps the older writers had, perhaps unwillingly. A lot of these writings seemed to be influenced by the parties backing the kings they were being written about. A lot of the recorded history may subtly have been party propaganda.

During this 100 year period I am writing about, from 1450s to 1550s, there is no shortage of historians' and chroniclers' works to read. Some formally educated in the church and some not so educated, all trying to make a name for themselves. Many of them learned quickly that if they wanted to do this, they had to become partisan. Many historians of that day had to write the history the way the kings and queens wanted it written or else life could be tough. Some writers didn't like certain kings and/or their queens and their families. When a certain historian didn't like a certain king or his family or anyone associated with them, I found that is generally where the rumours would start. If the writers were successful and gained a following, then the rumours would, after being believed long enough, be added to the annals of past history and their truth perhaps never challenged. The writers of that day didn't necessarily have to believe what they were writing as long as they could live comfortably and stay in the good graces of those who they were writing for.

In school when I studied logic, I was taught that if your conclusion is based on a false premise, then your conclusion will also be false as well. The late fifteenth century of English history is very poorly documented. Few contemporary chronicles survive today and some await examination. Much of what is known comes from later sources. For the years 1483–85 there are very few reliable contemporary sources.

Some of the historians of that day who managed to make a name for themselves I will mention here. The historian Dominic Mancini published a work known as *The Occupation of the Throne of England by Richard III*. This publication supposedly was well written and truthful. Before it could be read by other famous historians of his time, it was lost and wasn't discovered again until 1934, where it was discovered in a small library in France. Mancini had gone to England in 1482 with the French ambassador. He had been a monk in Italy and was well educated in the church. I am not certain how his work was influenced by his religious background. He was a prolific historian and did some fine work.

The movements of Richard, as documented by Mancini, had established the fact that indeed Richard was able to meet young Edward on his way to London to be crowned as king. That was some of the best chronicled writing I was able to read for this manuscript. In his writing, he was not judgmental of Richard. He left England shortly after Richard's coronation. He died in France in 1494.[2]

Other historians, such as Polydore Vergil and Sir Thomas More, knew of Mancini's book about how Richard III became king, but they didn't get a chance to read or study it because it had been lost. However, Mancini was still known and well respected by the historians and chroniclers of his time.[3] Another source for accurate history of the period 1483–85 is from the *Croyland Chronicle*. Several chronicles of English history were written at Croyland Abbey, a religious foundation in Lincolnshire. Some of the authors of the *Croyland Chronicle* were displeased by Richard III's behavior. The *Chronicle* did produce a large volume of history, by different writers, that was some of the most reliable of its time.[4]

As soon as King Richard III was dead and King Henry VII took his place on the throne, he demanded all copies of the *Act of Settlement* known as *Titulus Regius* (1484) be destroyed. This document outlined Richard III's title to the throne. Many copies of the manuscript of this Act were destroyed. King Henry had made it a criminal offense to have a copy of it in a person's possession. A few copies had survived, being hidden away. The Croyland manuscript was not used as a historical source until 1619. In 1731, that copy was badly burned.[5]

Another writer/historian of this time was John Rous. In his lifetime, 1411–1491, he was a Warwickshire chantry priest. Again, he too was educated in the church. It was believed he was not an eyewitness of a lot of the events he describes and was also known to record rumor as fact. Rous' work showed how Henry VII kingship, 1485–1509, affected the documentation of the history during his reign. Rous wrote a history of England dedicated to Henry VII in 1490. In this history Rous does not portray Richard III favorably. He believed he had killed Ann Neville, his wife and Queen.[6]

Polydore Vergil was an historian and a cleric, educated in the church, from Urbino, Italy. He came to England in 1501–02 and lived there for years. He became a Renaissance scholar. Henry VII wanted to use his historical talents and rewarded him well.[7]

Vergil was commissioned to write an official history of England. It took him nineteen years to complete twenty-six books in the Anglica Historia. It was published in 1534 in Basle. Vergil's history of Richard III's reign became known as the most detailed account of his time to be printed.

When necessary, Vergil could suppress the truth. He knew how not to offend the royal patrons, a policy supposedly adopted from his work by Henry VII himself.[8]

Sir Thomas More wrote a biography, *The History of King Richard III*, in 1514-18. More's account was from eye-witness detail. His historical writings have been criticized for having some incorrect names and dates. Some of his writings may not have been based on accurate sources. His writing has been verified by other sources, such as Mancini and Croyland, who were not known to More and Vergil.

More's history of Richard III was known to exhibit truthfulness and his intellectual judgment. The fate of the princes in the tower was his central theme. An Elizabethan scholar, Roger Ascham, described the book as a model of historical writing.

More was accused of writing propaganda for the Tudors. Henry VII in 1504 charged him of high treason for opposing him in Parliament. Henry realized that Thomas could not pay the fine, so he imprisoned and fined his father, Judge Sir John More. Henry VIII valued his opinion as an honest man. Later, More would not condone Henry VIII's break with Rome and was executed in 1535. Later he was proclaimed a saint by the Roman Catholic Church.

Sir George Buck was from an old Yorkist family. In 1619, Buck wrote and published *The History of King Richard III*. This writing was researched from some of the manuscripts that had been preserved.[9]

Sir Francis Bacon (1561-1626) published his work *The History of Henry VII* in 1622. Bacon was a lawyer, statesman and Lord Chancellor. His biography of Henry was considered well-researched, objective, and advanced for its time. He had an advantage of access to records that no longer exist.[10]

CHAPTER TWENTY

Titulus Regius: The Act Of Settlement

The English document *Titulus Regius*, meaning "royal title," also known as the *Act of Settlement*, was a statute of the Parliament of England, issued in 1484, by which the title of King of England was given to Richard III. It is an official declaration that describes why the Parliament had found in 1483 that the marriage of Edward IV to Elizabeth Woodville had been invalid, and consequently their children, Edward V and Richard of Shrewsbury, 1st Duke of York, as well as their eldest daughter Elizabeth, who became the wife of Henry VII, were illegitimate and debarred from the throne. Richard III was then proclaimed the rightful king.[1]

The above statement only covers one part of the document itself. In the expanded excerpt in the Author's Documents, it shows "Dame Elianor Butteler, as being married to King Edward, in a precontract of matronie." Then it followed that Edward IV and Elizabeth's marriage was considered illegal because Edward was already married to Lady Eleanor, so their children were judged to all be bastards.[2]

The Act was repealed by the first parliament of the new king, Henry VII. Henry then ordered his subjects to destroy all copies of the Act without reading it. So well were his orders carried out only one copy of the law has ever been found. A copy was transcribed by a monastic chronicler into the *Croyland Chronicle*, where it was discovered by historian Sir George Buck more than a century later during the reign of James I.[3]

I had first found Lady Eleanor Talbot-Butler's name in a book I was studying. It took me days to find the right years and the right characters I was searching for. I had seen Richard and James Tyrrell in the first dream but I wouldn't know who they were until I had done more research and found them in the same volume as Lady Eleanor. I knew instinctively this was the "Eleanor" I had been looking for. Her name jumped out at me and I knew she was one of the main characters in my dreams.[4]

The most shocking part of this finding was suddenly realizing that this women in my dreams was now present in books of history. This was a history I had purposely skipped over all my life. Even from a distance, this history looked too complicated to me and I just tried to ignore it and just forget about it. This Eleanor had been a real active part of that era. She was a real person. I had a hard time believing this was possible but there she was, in an actual historical publication.

Here was a woman that I had never heard anything about until she introduced herself to young Edward de Wigmore in my dreams, which really got me going on this project. I had already learned so much from the experiences of the dreams. However, it did take me a long time to actually sit down and begin. I now had to put the pieces, from both history and the dreams, in place in this manuscript. It is still taking me a long time to finish it, because I am still learning more of the written history as I go along. Every time I run across a new aspect of the history I'm writing about here, I try to weave it into the fabric of this story.

Lady Eleanor Talbot-Butler was spotlighted in the famous English document *Titulus Regius*. When I saw a copy of that document, I knew my dream concerned a part of actual English history. I knew then for sure that I wanted to pursue this research.

As I have mentioned above, this state document entitled *Titulus Regius* had been passed by King Richard's Parliament in 1484, which set forth Richard III's title to the throne. In August of 1485, Richard was killed in a battle at Bosworth Field.

In November 1485, as soon as Henry VII officially became king he demanded *Titulus Regius* be removed from the Statute Books and any documents referring to the Act destroyed. By government order, anyone found with a copy of it was required to return it to Henry's government by Easter of 1486. Anyone found with a copy of it after that time period could be imprisoned and fined. Very few people had any idea what that document had stated or why it needed to be destroyed.

John Speed, an English historian found a copy of *Titulus Regius* in 1611. The people could finally realize what that document meant to the history of that era. It was too late for anyone to voice an opinion of it, but it did show that Henry VII had gotten what he wanted. The persons or issues this document was concerned with were forgotten and left out of the history for the time being.[5]

Henry wanted to marry Elizabeth, Edward's daughter, but they were both descendants of Edward III. They were closely related but were not forbidden to marry. Henry worried though that there might be objections from the Earl of Warwick, because he was the last direct descendant of Edward III.[6]

When Henry became king, he knew there were certain people who might protest his kingship. He began by putting young Earl of Warwick away for good. Henry had Bishop Stillington, the man who married Edward IV and Lady Eleanor, arrested because Henry blamed him for making up the "precontract" story and had caused his Queen to be labeled a bastard. After *Titulus Regius* was repealed, Stillington was pardoned. William Catesby, who is in my family tree, served in Richard III's kingship and was executed when Henry took office. It seems no one was let go that had served in Richard III's short term as king.[7]

CHAPTER TWENTY-ONE
Henry VII: His Dreams Of Kingship

D avid Williamson, in his publication *History of the Kings &*
Queens of England, characterized Henry VII as follows:

Henry Tudor was the only child of Edmond Tudor, Earl of
Richmond (one of the half-brothers of Henry VI), and his
wife Lady Margaret Beaufort, in her turn the only child
of John Beaufort, Duke of Somerset, grandson of John of
Gaunt, Duke of Lancaster, the fourth son of Edward III.
He was born to his 13-year-old mother at Pembrook Castle
in January 1457, three months after the death of his father,
whom he succeeded as Earl of Richmond at birth.

The infant Henry and his mother lived under the protection of his uncle Jasper Tudor, son of Henry V's
widow Cathrine and Owen Tudor. As Constable for the
Lancastrian Tudors he held Pembroke Castle until it was
captured for the Yorkists by Lord Herbert in 1461. The
change in ownership made little difference to Henry's life,
Lord and Lady Herbert being kind foster parents.

The "readaption" of Henry VI in 1470 brought Jasper Tudor
back to Pembrook to fetch his nephew to court and there
is a tradition that Henry attended his royal half-uncle's
foundation at Eton. If so, it could have only been for a very
short time as he returned to Wales with Jasper in 1471.

After the Lancastrian defeats at Barnet and Tewkesbury. Pembrook was besieged, but the Tudors, uncle and nephew, were helped to escape and sailed from Tenby en route to France. Stormy weather drove them ashore in Brittany, where they were hospitably received by the Duke. They remained in Brittany for 13 years, successfully evading all attempts to extradite them.

Genealogically, Henry VII's claim to the throne was very tenuous as he was descended from John of Gaunt's third marriage to Catherine Swynford, which had taken place after the birth of their children. These were subsequently legitimized but their ineligibility for succession to the throne was later added to the Act of Legitimization.[1]

Immediately after the victory of Bosworth Field, Henry proceeded to London and was crowned at Westminster Abbey on 30 October 1485. The following month Parliament passed an act confirming Henry's right to the throne and settling it on his legitimacy issue. He was further petitioned by the Lords and Commons to marry Elizabeth of York, the eldest daughter of Edward IV, which he did at Westminster on 18 January 1486. Apart from considering himself the lawful heir of the House of Lancaster and being married to the lawful heiress of the House of York, Henry also laid claim to a much older tradition. Through his Welsh grandfather he traced his descent from ancient British kings and saw himself as the lawful successor of the legendary King Arthur. He gave the name of Arthur to his first born son and adopted the red dragon of Wales as one of his supporters of the royal arms

Henry had to contend with two pretenders to the throne: Lambert Simnel, who claimed to be Earl of Warwick, son of George, Duke of Clarence, and Perkin Warbeck, who pretended to be Richard, Duke of York, the younger son of Edward IV. Both were dealt with satisfactorily; the former was pardoned and lived for many years working as a turn spite in the royal kitchens; the latter was imprisoned in the Tower and eventually hanged after an attempted escape.

Henry brought peace and prosperity to the country after many years of civil strife. He was parsimonious by nature, but maintained a splendid court and spent lavishly on building projects, rebuilding Baynard's Castle and Greenwich Palace, building a new palace at Richmond upon Thames to replace the old Sheen Palace, and adding the exquisite Lady Chapel, which has come to be known as Henry VII Chapel, to Westminster Abbey. He also founded several religious houses and supported his mother's religious and educational foundations.

Henry arranged a grand royal marriage for his eldest son Arthur, Prince of Wales, with the Infanta Catherine of Aragon, the youngest daughter of the Spanish sovereigns, Fernando II of Aragon and Isabel of Castile. It took place at St. Paul's Cathedral on 14 November 1501, but in the following year Arthur fell ill with the sweating sickness, and died at Ludlow Castle on 2 April, leaving Catherine a childless widow. His death was a great blow to his parents and Queen Elizabeth herself died in childbirth at the Tower of London on her 37th birthday, 11 February 1503.

Henry contemplated remarrying from time to time, but never actually did so. His own health was poor and he suffered from gout and asthma. He died at Richmond Palace on 21 April 1509, aged 52.

In retrospect, during the early years of Henry's reign, he knew he had to build up his image, so one narrative piece that I liked and decided to use was written by Polydore Vergil, entitled *Anglica Historia*, and it reads a follows:[2]

His body was slender but well built and strong; his height above the average. His appearance was remarkably attractive and his face was cheerful, especially when speaking; his eyes were small and blue, his teeth few, poor and blackish; his hair was thin and white; his complexion sallow. His spirit was distinguished, wise and prudent; his mind was brave and resolute and never, even at moments of the greatest danger, deserted him. He had a most pertinacious memory. Withal he was not devoid of scholarship. In government he was shrewd and prudent, so that no one dared to get the better of him through deceit or guile. He was gracious and kind and was as attentive to his visitors as he was of access. His hospitality was splendidly generous; he was fond of having foreigners at his court and he freely conferred favors of them. But those of his subjects who were indebted to him and who did not pay him due honor or who were generous only with promises, he treated with harsh severity. He well knew how to maintain his royal majesty and all which appertains to kingship at every time and in every place. He was most fortunate in war, although he was constitutionally more inclined to peace than to war. He cherished justice above all things; as a result he vigorously punished violence, manslaughter and every other kind of wickedness whatsoever, consequently he was greatly regretted on that account by all his subjects, who had been able to conduct their lives peaceably, far removed from the assaults and evil doing of scoundrels. He was the most ardent supporter of our faith, and daily participated with great piety in religious services. To those whom he considered to be worthy priests, he often secretly gave alms so that they should pray for his salvation. He was particularly fond of those Franciscan friars whom they call Observants, for whom he founded many convents, so that with his help their rule should continually flourish in his kingdom, but all these virtues were obscured latterly only by avarice, from which he suffered. This avarice is surely a bad enough vice in a private individual, whom it forever torments; in a monarch indeed it may be considered the worst vice, since it is harmful to everyone, and distorts those qualities of trustfulness, justice and integrity by which the state must be governed.

Author's Conclusion

R ecording events that cause other events to happen is not history. The records of the causes of events is the true task of the historian and history. Because there may not be enough applicable and reliable information to draw from to form a final opinion, the true history of nations may never be told.

The young historians of today have to be able to pull apart the shreds of the history that still remain and try to make some logical conclusions from whatever they can discover. If there are not enough of the real facts of an important historical event then a solid conclusion can't be reached. The history that is being recorded then becomes a series of guesses. Who is to say if the conclusion is right or wrong?

When historical events are even partially censored by governments, or their successors, then historians should begin to rely on their own interpretations of why and how particular historical events take place.

When the blank pages of history become filled with rumours, if they are repeated often enough, just like in small communities where everyone knows each other, those rumours will eventually become known as the truth.

My method of writing this history is based on sheer common sense. I read the history, whether it is directly from that era or works of contemporary writers. If the writing doesn't fit with the historical facts I have already collected, I explore the reasoning of why it was written that way. So far that method has lead me to some interesting conclusions.

Our knowledge is based mostly on theories. If these theories can't be proven because of the lack of facts then how solid is our knowledge and how true is the history?

I have experienced this same problem with what I am writing here. I didn't have any previous prejudice toward any of the sources I referenced in writing this manuscript. At first I believed them all. It didn't take me long, after reading a good cross section of the historians' writings on this part of English history, to form a different opinion.

I believe now some of this history was written in such a convoluted fashion to purposely confuse the historians and chroniclers. If the history confused those people who worked with it as a profession, then it would be likely that ordinary people would find it "over their head" and not concern themselves with it unless it began to affect their lives in a drastic way. Issues that should have been delved into and explored were being put away out of the public view and quickly forgotten.

Historians of today need to become "historical detectives." If there is doubt about the truthfulness of an historical event(s), they must be able to take the information they find and take it apart piece by piece and explore it. If there is truth to be found, then find it.

Author's Notes

CHAPTER ONE

[1] Edgar Allan Poe, *Sixty-Seven Tales*, p. 718.

[2] Alison Weir, *The Princes in the Tower*, p. 118. This was one of only a few references I researched that mentioned Sudeley Castle, Lady Eleanor Talbot-Butler and Edward de Wigmore.

[3] W.E. Wightman, "The Palatine Earldom of William fitz Osbern in Gloucestershire (1066-1071)," *English Historical Review* (1962), pp. 6–17.

[4] David Ross, Britain Express, Cheltenham, UK. See page 206.

CHAPTER TWO

[1] The field I found my arrowheads on was also part of the fields that battles of the American Civil War were fought on. From that experience, I went on to study history at university.

CHAPTER THREE

No entries.

CHAPTER FOUR

[1] Coat of Arms: Paget/Boddie family histories, ©1994. Published by "The Hall of Names" Inc., US and Canada.

[2] The Coat of Arms mentioned above showed me that my two ancestral families had known each other at least since 1066.

[3] The Pagets were living on the Isle of Menorca in the 1350s. They were one of the families that settled there and were trading with the far east.

[4] Anthony Paget settled in the Virginia Colony in 1623 and was a founding member of the governing body known as "The House of Burgesses" in 1629. William Paget was a sponsor for the Virginia expedition for settlement. Thomas Paget settled there in 1643. William Boddie, of my grand-mother's family, brought colonists to the Virginia colony and helped establish the tobacco and cotton trade there. Some of this information was provided by The Colonial Williamsburg Foundation, Williamsburg, Virginia.

[5] Historians at the University of Richmond, Virginia, explained that the slave peoples that were brought there spoke dialects from Ivory Coast in West Africa, known as 'gulla' and 'gettche.' They used these dialects so they could converse with one another without being understood by the slave owners.

[6] Boddie family papers, UK.

[7] The slave trade caused a marked increase in tribal warfare in West Africa, in order to take more captives to sell into slavery.

[8] Boddie family papers, UK.

[9] Tony Mack McClure, PhD, *Cherokee Proud*, p. 193.

[10] Paget family papers, UK.

[11] ibid.

[12] Boddie family papers, UK.

[13] Edmund H. Fellowes, *The Knights of the Garter, 1348–1939*.

CHAPTER FIVE

[1] See page 211.

[2] David Ross, Britain Express, Cheltenham, UK.

[3] This drawing of the floor plan of de Wigmore Castle from my dreams. See page 210.

[4] Alison Weir, *The Princes in the Tower*, p. 118.

[5] David Ross, Britain Express, Cheltenham, UK.

[6] David Ross, Britain Express, Cheltenham, UK. Real estate record of ownership of Sudeley Castle from 1066-1472. See page 206.

[7] Richard Jones and John Mason, *Haunted Castles of Britain and Ireland*, p. 39.

[8] David Ross, Britain Express, Cheltenham, UK. Real estate record of ownership of Sudeley Castle. See page 206.

[9] Alison Weir, *The Princes in the Towers*, pp. 119-120.

[10] Alison Weir, *Britain's Royal Family: A Complete Genealogy*.

[11] Edmund H. Fellowes, *The Knights of the Garter, 1348–1939*, p. 29.

[12] See letter page 212.

[13] David Ross, Britain Express, Cheltenham, UK. Real estate record of ownership of Sudeley Castle from 1066-1472. See page 206.

[14] ibid.

CHAPTER SIX

[1] W.E. Wightman's article "The Palatine Earldom of William fitz Osbern in Gloucestershire and Worcestershire (1066-1071)" stated that Earl William had built de Wigmore Castle. That proved to me there was a connection between the de Wigmore family and his family. I believe then Jane de Wigmore was related to the FitzOsberne family by marriage many years back.

CHAPTER SEVEN

[1] David Williamson, *Kings and Queens of England*, p. 55. An explanation of who Sir James Tyrrell was and what his fate was. I believe he took the fall for other persons' crimes.

CHAPTER EIGHT

No entries.

CHAPTER NINE

[1] I could not understand why Lady Eleanor would have married Edward IV. Her family had already been killed off under Edward's rule. The written history states she went to see if she could get her properties back. Edward married her and later she was put under house arrest.

[2] It took me awhile to understand why they had exchanged babies. I believe that move saved young Edward's life.

[3] I want you to know now that I later came to disagree with Jane's depiction of Eleanor's incarceration. I explain my rationale about this in Chapter Fifteen (see page 145).

[4] Edward IV did not like to be outsmarted and would find ways to get even. He was a vindictive person.

CHAPTER TEN

[1] Much of the information in the dreams came to me in a nonlinear format. The *symbolic codes* was an expression I used to describe how certain information served as a subtle catalyst to lead me from one historical event to the other. Sometimes these historical findings were in conflict with each other and I used these codes to sort those conflicts into the sequence they needed to be in.

[2] I believe young Edward de Wigmore was named by his mother

and Jane de Wigmore, and not by Edward IV. He would not have named this child after a new found enemy. He went to de Wigmore Castle to find that son and have him put away. He did not care what that child's name was.

[3] In *The Princes in the Tower*, p. 118, Alison Weir explained that the older British historian, Sir George Buck, had stated Lady Eleanor Talbot was said to have had a male child by Edward IV. He explains the child was known as Edward de Wigmore and was supposed to have been the great-grandfather of Richard Wigmore who had worked as a secretary in Elizabeth I's government. I saw that as a possibility that young Edward did not die in infancy.

[4] William FitzOsberne, 1st Earl of Hereford and castle builder to William I, in UK from 1066 to 1071, or 1087. Historical dates are wrong here for his son and himself and I could not establish why. I suspect they were both murdered because they were becoming too wealthy and politically powerful. Richard Jones, in his book *Haunted Castles of Britain and Ireland*, mentions that Earl William was working on Norwich Castle in 1087. All the other resources I used stated he died in 1071 fighting in France.

[5] My drawing of de Wigmore Castle was from the layout of it in my dreams. That was the only information I had available to draw my floor plan from so far. See page 210.

CHAPTER ELEVEN

[1] *Keys and fragments* is one of the literary tools I developed to help identify certain information I needed for this type of writing.

[2] The image of Lady Eleanor for the cover of my publication is a portrait painted by Teresa Marie. The pose is of her sitting in Sudeley Castle facing Edward IV asking him to have her properties redocumented in her name.

[3] David Williamson, *History of the Kings & Queens of England*, p. 54. Author's comment: This was one of my main resources that would mention Lady Eleanor.

[4] It was at this point I finally realized Lady Eleanor Butler (Talbot) had been left out of this period of history. She was the Queen of England for some three years, from 1461 to 1464.

[5] Alison Weir, *The Princes in the Tower*, p. 118. This was the first time I saw Lady Eleanor mentioned in an historical publication in relation to Edward IV. That was a real shock!

[6] ibid, *Titulus Regius*, p. 117.

[7] Alison Weir, *The Princes in the Tower*, p. 118.

[8] ibid, pg. 120.

[9] ibid, pp. 117–120.

[10] David Williamson, *The Kings & Queens of England*, p. 57.

[11] Alison Weir, *The Princes in the Tower*, p. 223.

[12] ibid, pg. 120.

CHAPTER TWELVE

[1] Alison Weir, *The Princes in the Tower*, p. 118.

[2] Why would Edward go looking for their son at de Wigmore Castle and put Eleanor under house arrest if their marriage was not legal and if their son was not of legitimate birth and still alive?

[3] Denise Lynn, *Past Lives, Present Dreams*, pp. 1–5, 121.

[4] Denise Lynn, *The Hidden Powers of Dreams*, pp. 14–16.

[5] Our dreams are not considered real, so I had to find where my dreams matched the "real history."

[6] Later on in the history of the Middle Ages, original copies of the document *Titulus Regius* did begin to surface. This document again showed proof for the third time that Edward IV was legally married to Lady Eleanor Talbot-Butler. Why else would Richard III have gone to all that trouble to get *T. Regius* passed?

[7] David Williamson, *History of the Kings & Queens of England*, p. 60.

[8] Lady Eleanor is not mentioned or alluded to in William

Shakespeare's play, *Richard III*. King Edward's other wife, Elizabeth Woodville, is one of the main characters. The tall soldier that told me not to go upstairs in my first dream was Sir James Tyrrell, trainer and bodyguard to young King Richard.

[9] Denise Lynn, *The Hidden Power of Dreams*, pp. 90–91.

[10] ibid, p. 28.

[11] ibid, p. 51.

[12] ibid, p. 89.

[13] ibid, p. 90.

[14] ibid, p. 91.

CHAPTER THIRTEEN

[1] David Williamson, *History of the Kings & Queens of England*, pp. 53–55.

[2] Charles Ross, *Edward IV*, p. 274.

[3] Edmund H. Fellowes, *The Knights of the Garter*, (1348–1939).

[4] Charles Ross, *Edward IV*, p. 33.

[5] ibid, p. 34.

[6] ibid, p. 75.

[7] ibid, p. 376.

[8] David Williamson, *History of the Kings & Queens of England*, p. 54. To clarify, the "12-year-old Prince Edward" referred to here was Elizabeth's child.

CHAPTER FOURTEEN

[1] William of Tyre, *Historia and Old French Continuation*.

[2] Thomas B. Costain, *The Three Edwards*, pp. 263, 437, 441.

[3] Michael Baigent, et al., *Holy Blood, Holy Grail*, p. 241.

[4] David Williamson, *History of the Kings & Queens of England*, p. 27.

[5] ibid, p. 25.

[6] ibid, pp. 36–43. Historian David Williamson classified the Plantagenet rule from 1216–1327

[7] Edmund H. Fellowes, *The Knights of the Garter, 1348–1939*. p. 9.

[8] Charles Ross, *Edward IV*, p. 102.

CHAPTER FIFTEEN

[1] Alison Weir, *The Princes in the Tower*, p. 21. This source claims Edward married Elizabeth Woodville in the spring of 1464 at Grafton Manor, attended by Elizabeth's mother, the Duchess of Bedford, and a priest and three witnesses.

[2] ibid, p. 45.

[3] David Williamson, *History of the Kings & Queens of England*, p. 53.

[4] In the above statement there was no mention of a priest or witnesses being present. Under English law at that time, I believe this marriage should not have been considered legal.

[5] David Ross, Britain Express, Cheltenham, Gloucestershire, UK.

[6] Richard Jones, and photos by John Mason, *Haunted Castles of Britain and Ireland*, p. 39.

[7] Charles Ross, *Edward IV*, p. 203. I am not sure how Sir Thomas Butler died. The written history had conflicting stories on this issue. Here my dreams differed in cause and place of death.

[8] Lady Eleanor had a dream that young Edward would be king someday.

[9] Alison Weir, *The Princes in the Tower*, p. 45.

[10] David Williamson, *History of the Kings & Queens of England*, p. 53.

[11] Alison Weir, *The Princes in the Tower*, p. 118.

[12] Charles Ross, *Edward IV*, p. 3. I believe the dates of the birth of young Edward are wrong here. According to the written history,

Edward married Elizabeth Woodville in May of 1464. Then it states Lady Eleanor birthed young Edward de Wigmore in 1468 and they both died shortly afterwards at the Carmelite Church in Norwich. Maybe the dates were wrong for a reason. This alludes to the fact that Edward may not have been the father of Lady Eleanor's son and could have possibly cleared his name of that affair! Then my question is why was the *Titulus Regius* banned by Henry VII in 1485? To answer my own question, I sincerely believe young Edward was still out there somewhere. He would have been seventeen years old when Henry became king in 1485. He could have still challenged Henry for the kingship.

[13] See page 212.

CHAPTER SIXTEEN

[1] Edmund H. Fellowes, *The Knights of the Garter, 1348-1939*.

[2] ibid, p. x.

[3] Charles Ross, *Edward IV*, p. 274.

[4] ibid, p. 33.

[5] ibid, p. 34.

[6] This statement is conjecture on my part.

[7] David Williamson, *King and Queens of England*, p. 54.

[8] Edmund H. Fellowes, *The Knights of the Garter, 1348–1939*.

CHAPTER SEVENTEEN

[1] Charles Ross, *Edward IV*, p. 97.

[2] ibid, pp. 414-16.

[3] ibid, p. 414.

[4] Edward Hall, *Croyland Chronicle*, no. 18, p. 555.

[5] Dominic Mancini (Italian historian), *Croyland Chronicle*, p. 59.

[6] Philippe de Commynes, *Croyland Chronicle*, p. 304.

[7] Charles Ross, *Edward IV*, p. 414.

[8] ibid, p. 415.

[9] Mrs. M. Grieve, *A Modern Herbal*, p. 391.

[10] Charles Ross, *Edward IV*, p. 416.

[11] David Williamson, *History of The Kings & Queens of England*, p. 54.

[12] Winston Churchill, *The History of the English Speaking Peoples*, p. 377.

[13] David Williamson, *History of The Kings & Queens of England*, p. 54.

CHAPTER EIGHTEEN

[1] Charles Ross, *Edward IV*. p. 97.

[2] ibid, p. 97.

[3] ibid, p. 87.

[4] D. MacGibbon, *Elizabeth Woodville*, p. 225.

[5] David Williamson, *History of the Kings & Queens of England*, p. 55.

[6] David Ross, Britain Express, Cheltenham, UK.

[7] Edmund H. Fellowes, *The Knights of the Garter, 1348–1939*, p. 37.

[8] William Shakespeare, from the play, *Richard III*, edited by Mark Eccles, 1964, 1988, Penguin.

CHAPTER NINETEEN

[1] Alison Weir, *The Princes in the Tower*, p. 17.

[2] ibid, pp. 2–3.

[3] ibid, p. 3.

[4] *The Croyland Chronicle*

[5] ibid.

[6] Alison Weir, *The Princes in the Tower*, p. 6.

[7] ibid, pp. 7–8.

[8] ibid, p. 8.

[9] Sir George Buck, *The History of King Richard III*, c. 1619.

[10] Sir Francis Bacon, *The History of King Henry VII*, c. 1622.

CHAPTER TWENTY

[1] *Titulus Regius*, "The Act of Settlement" (1484).

[2] ibid.

[3] *Croyland Chronicle* and historian Sir George Buck (senior), circa 1620.

[4] Alison Weir, *The Princes in the Tower*, pp. 117–18.

[5] ibid, p. 219.

[6] ibid, p. 11.

[7] ibid, p. 220.

CHAPTER TWENTY-ONE

[1] David Williamson, *History of the Kings & Queens of England*, pp. 51–61.

[2] Polydore Vergil, *The Anglica Historia*, translated and edited by D. Hay, Camden Series (1950).

Select Bibliography

GENERAL SOURCES

Bridgeford, Andrew. 1066, *The Hidden History of the Bayeux Tapestry.* 4th Estate, 2004.

Plas Newydd. National Trust Booklet, 1976. This booklet shows a small part of my great-grandmother's family history. Her name was Ellen Griffith of Penrhyn. The Griffith name came from a man named Gwilym ap Gruffydd (1376–1431). Gwilym's wife Morfudd was the daughter of Goronwy Fychan of Penmynydd.

Poe, Edgar Allan. "A Dream Within A Dream." *Sixty-Seven Tales.* p. 718. Avenel, New Jersey: Outlet Book Co., 1985

EDWARD IV SOURCES

Clive, Mary M. *This Sun of York; A Biography of Edward IV.* MacMillan, 1973.

Commines, Philippe de. *Mémoires.* Ed. Andrew Scobie, 1900, and J. Calmette and G. Durville, 3 vols. Paris: 1924–25.

Costain, Thomas B. *A History of the Plantagenets: The Three Edwards.* New York: Doubleday, 1962.

Fellowes, Edmund H. *The Knights of the Garter.* London: The Society for Promoting Christian Knowledge, 1939.

Grieve, M. *A Modern Herbal.* New York: Dover, 1931.

Jenkins, Elizabeth. *The Princes in the Tower.* New York: Coward, McCann, Geoghegan Inc., 1978

Jones, Richard. *Haunted Castles of Britain and Ireland.* New York: Barnes and Noble, 2003.

Lander, J.R. *Conflict and Stability in 15th Century England.* London: Hutchinson, 1969

Lander, J.R. *The Wars of the Roses.* London: Sutton, 1990.

O'Brien, J., Mark Harbison. *Ancient Ireland from Prehistory to the Middle Ages.* Oxford University Press, 1996.

Ormrod, W.M. *The Kings and Queens of England.* Port Stroud, UK: Tempus Publishing, 2001.

Penman, Sharon Kay. *Here Be Dragons.* New York: Ballantine, 1985.

The Atlas of World History. Rand McNally, 1957.

Ross, Charles. *Edward IV.* Berkeley: University of California Press, 1976.

Scofield, Cora L. *The Life and Reign of Edward IV.* Two volumes. Frank Case & Co.,1967.

Vergil, Polydore. *Three Books of Polydore Vergil's English History.* H.C. Maxwell Lyte (ed.). Camden Society, 1937.

Warkworth, John D. *Three Chronicles of the Reign of Edward IV.* Keith Dockray (introduction). Gloucester: Sutton, 1988.

Weir, Alison. *The Princes in the Tower.* London: Pimlico, 1993.

Williamson, David. *History of the Kings & Queens of England.* New York: Konecky and Konecky, 1998.

RICHARD III SOURCES

Buck, Sir George. *History of the Life & Reign of Richard III.* Sutton, 1979.

Drewitt, Richard, Mark Redhead. *The Trial of Richard lll.* Sutton, 1984.

Eccles, Mark. *Richard III by William Shakespeare.* New York: New American Library, 1964.

Gairdner, James. *The Letters & Papers of the Reign of Richard III & Henry VII.* Two volumes. Rolls Series, 1861-63.

Hanham, Alison. *Richard III and His Early Historians, 1483-1535.* Alan & Unwin, 1960.

Kendall, Paul Murray. *Richard III.* Alan & Unwin, 1965.

Kendall, Paul Murray. *The Yorkest Age*. Alan & Unwin, 1962.

Levine, Mortimer. *Richard III—Usurper or Lawful King*. Speculum, 1959.

More, Sir Thomas. *The History of King Richard III* (Vol. 2). Richard Sylvester (ed.). Yale University Press, 1963.

Myers, A.R. *Richard III, English Historical Document*. Eyers & Spottiswoode, 1969.

Potter, Jeremy. *Good King Richard*. Constable, 1983.

Ross, Charles. *Richard III*. Eyre & Methune, 1981.

Rowse, A.L. *Bosworth Field and the Wars of the Roses*. MacMillian, 1966.

Woodward, G.W.O. *King Richard III*. Pitkin, 1972.

LADY ELEANOR BUTLER (TALBOT) SOURCES

Boardman, A.E. *The Battle of Towton*. London: Stroud, 1994.

Cokayne, G.E.C. *The Complete Peerage; History of Lady Eleanor Talbot's Family*, London: 1910.

Pollard, A.J. *The Family of Talbot, Lords Talbot and Earls of Shrewsbury, in the 15th Century*. Bristol, UK: An unpublished thesis, 1968.

Weir, Alison. *The Princes in the Tower*. London: Pimlico, 1993.

PLANTAGENET SOURCES

Baigent, Michael, Richard Leigh, Henry Lincoln. *Holy Blood, Holy Grail*. New York: Dell, 1982.

Costain, Thomas B. *The Three Edwards: A History of the Plantagenets*. New York: Doubleday, 1962.

Fellowes, Edmund H. *The Knights of the Garter, 1348-1939*. London: The Society for Promoting Christian Knowledge, 1939.

Weir, Alison. *Britain's Royal Family: A Complete Genealogy*. p. 141. London: The Bodley Head, 1900

Williamson, David. *History of the Kings & Queens of England*. New York: Konecky and Konecky, 1998.

THE ORDER OF THE GARTER SOURCES

Baigent, Michael, Richard Leigh, Henry Lincoln. *Holy Blood, Holy Grail*. New York: Dell, 1982.

Costain, Thomas B. *The Three Edwards: A History of the Plantagenets.* New York: Doubleday, 1962.

Fellowes, Edmund H. *The Knights of the Garter, 1348-1939.* London: The Society for Promoting Christian Knowledge, 1939.

Ross, Charles. *Edward IV.* Berkeley and Los Angeles: University of California Press, 1974.

Weir, Alison. *The Princes in the Towers.* London: Pimlico, 1993.

PSYCHOLOGICAL SOURCES

Linn, Denise. *The Hidden Powers of Dreams.* New York: Ballantine, 1988.

Linn, Denise. *Past Lives, Present Dreams.* New York: Ballantine, 1997. Toronto: Random House, 1997.

Weiss, Brian L. *Through Time Into Healing.* New York: Simon and Schuster, 1992.

HENRY VII & ELIZABETH OF YORK SOURCES

Ross, Charles. *Edward IV.* Berkeley and Los Angeles: University of California Press, 1974.

Weir, Alison. *The Princes in the Tower.* London: Pimlico, 1993.

Williamson, David. *History of the Kings & Queens of England.* New York: Konecky and Konecky, 1998.

TITULUS REGIUS SOURCES

Titulus Regius, http://www.richard111.com/titulus_regius.htm, accessed on 6 December 2008.

Ross, Charles. *Edward IV.* Berkeley and Los Angeles: University of California Press, 1974.

Weir, Alison. *The Princes in the Towers.* London: Pimlico, 1993.

Author's Documents

The first document I present is the "Owners of Sudeley Castle" list. This document is included to show Edward IV became the owner of Sudeley Castle. Then it shows the castle was given to his brother, Richard, Duke of Gloucester, who later became Richard III.

The next document is a floor plan of Sudeley Castle that shows the old original floor plan or as close to the original as could be found.

These first two documents were obtained from David Ross, Britain Express at Lower Ground Floor, 85 London Road, Cheltenham, Gloucestershire, GL52-6HL.

The next document included is my drawing of the floor plan of Sudeley Castle, from the image of it in my dreams. This is to show how close my floor plan was after never having seen any floor plan of Sudeley Castle, previously.

The next document is my floor plan drawing of de Wigmore Castle. The main principle that my structural plan had in common with many of the older Welsh castles is the 'housed stables,' because they were used as fortresses to fight wars. I had never seen a floor plan of de Wigmore Castle, before I had drawn my drawing, once again from the image of it from my dreams. I still have not found a complete original floor plan of this castle.

The next three documents explain who Edward de Wigmore was. This information was taken from *rootsweb.ancestry.com* and *thepeerage.com* and from Alison Weir, *Britain's Royal Family: A Complete*

Genelogy (The Bodley Head: London, UK. 1999) p. 141.

I include a scan of the letter I received in 2003 from Sister Judith Leckie, Prioress of Carmel of our Lady of Walsingham convent in Langham, Norfolk, UK regarding whether or not Lady Eleanor Butler had been a resident at the convent in 1468.

Finally, I include an excerpt from the *Titulus Regius* containing the reference to "Dame Elianor Butteler" [*sic*]. The full text can be found at *http://www.richardiii.com/titulus_regius.htm.*

OWNERS OF SUDELEY CASTLE

Holders of the Manor or Castle of Sudeley since the Domesday Book

DATES	OWNER
prior to 1066	Ralph Medatine (or De Maunt) Earl of Hereford son – Harold, Lord Sudeley son – John de Sudeley son – Ralph de Sudeley son – Otnell de Sudeley (no issue)
c.1199	brother – Ralph de Sudeley
c.1222	son – Ralph de Sudeley
c.1267-1280	son – Bartholomew de Sudeley
c.1287-1337	John de Sudeley (no issue)
	nephew – John de Sudeley – m. Eleanor
– 1362	Eleanor
1362-1368	son – John de Sudeley
	sisters – Joan & Margery, who m. William le Boteler of Wem
1369-1399	son – Thomas le Boteler
	son – John (no issue)
1442	brother – Ralph, created Baron of Sudeley, built the castle at Sudeley
1469	castle & manor sold or forfeited to Edward IV
Manor granted to a succession of court favourites	
1469-1478	by Edward IV to Richard, Duke of Gloucester
1486-1495	by Henry VII to his uncle Jasper, Duke of Bedford, and his heirs male
1547	by Edward VI to Thomas, Lord Seymour (created Baron Sudeley)
1552	to William Parr, Marquis of Northampton (brother of Katherine Parr)
1554-1557	to Sir John Bridges (created Lord Chandos of Sudeley)
1562-1572	son – Edmund, Lord Chandos
1572-1594	son – Giles, Lord Chandos (no issue)
-1602	brother – William, by deed of entail
1602-1622	son – Grey, Lord Chandos (King of Cotswold)
1622-1654	son – George (sixth Lord Chandos)

OWNERS OF SUDELEY CASTLE

Holders of the Manor or Castle of Sudeley since the Domesday Book

DATES	OWNER
1654-	Jane, 2nd wife of George, m. George Pitt of Stratfield-Saye
-1694	George Pitt
1694-1734	son – George
1734-	son – George Pitt (created Baron Pitt in 1776)
1837	John and William Dent (brothers – no issue)
1855	nephew – John Dent, m. Emma Brocklehurst
-1900	Emma Dent
1900-1932	nephew – Henry Dent-Brocklehurst
1932-1949	son – JM Dent-Brocklehurst
1949-1972	son – Mark Dent-Brocklehurst (m. Elizabeth Chipps)
1972-	Elizabeth Brocklehurst m. Lord Ashcombe

Source: *http://www.britainexpress.com/counties/glouces/castles/sudeley-owners. htm* retrieved 22 December 2016, courtesy David Ross, Britain Express, used with permission.

ORIGINAL FLOOR PLAN OF SUDELEY CASTLE

Source: David Ross, Britain Express, February 2014

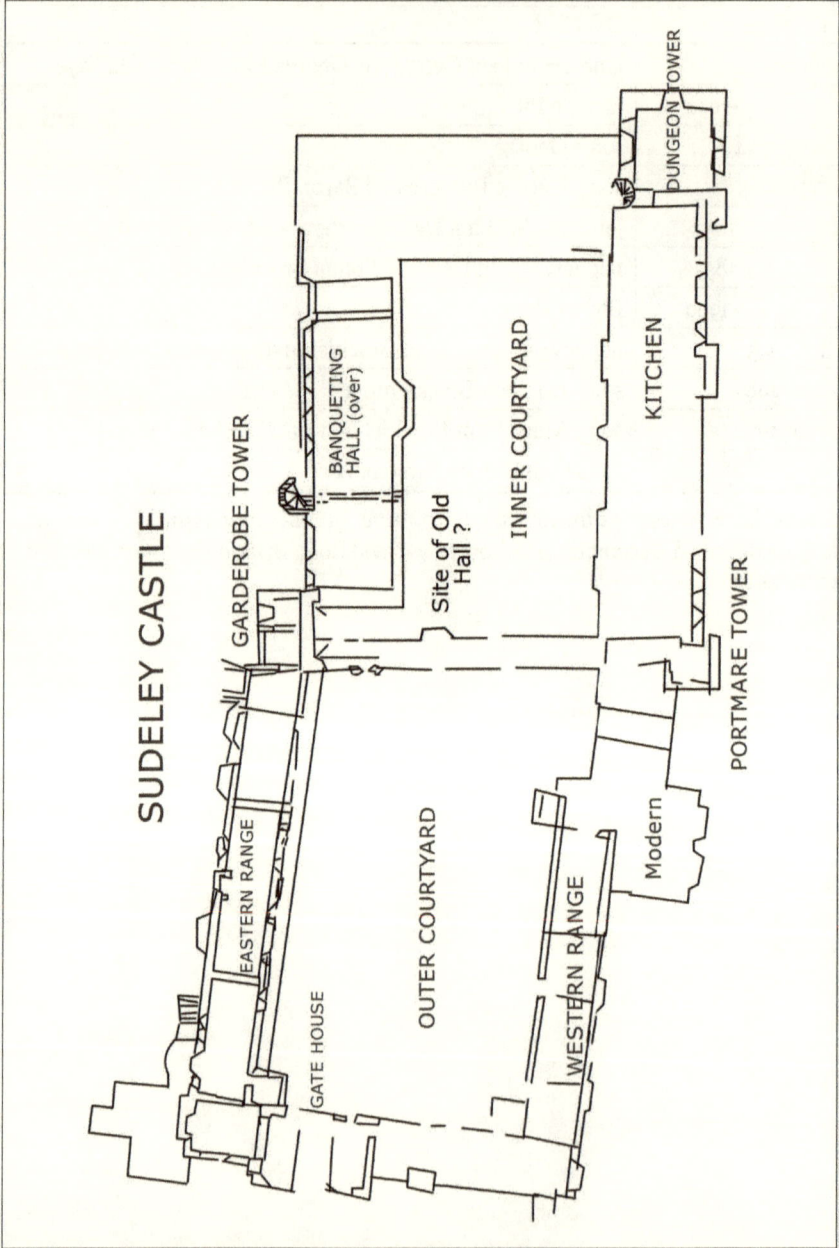

SUDELEY CASTLE

GARDEROBE TOWER

BANQUETING HALL (over)

Site of Old Hall ?

INNER COURTYARD

DUNGEON TOWER

KITCHEN

PORTMARE TOWER

EASTERN RANGE

OUTER COURTYARD

GATE HOUSE

Modern

WESTERN RANGE

FLOOR PLAN DRAWING OF SUDELEY CASTLE

Winchcombe, Gloucestershire, UK, from May 1468
© 1994, Clarence W. Padgett

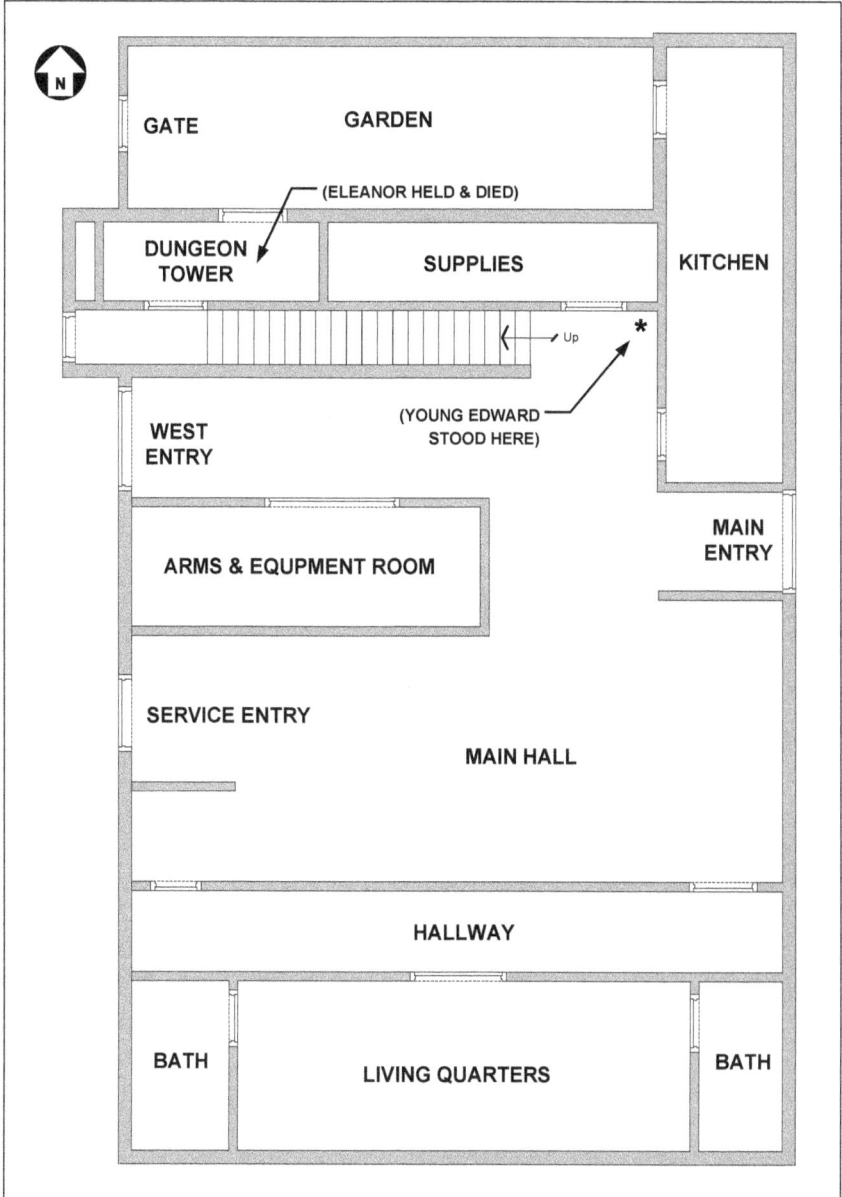

GATE

GARDEN

(ELEANOR HELD & DIED)

DUNGEON TOWER

SUPPLIES

KITCHEN

Up

(YOUNG EDWARD STOOD HERE)

*

WEST ENTRY

MAIN ENTRY

ARMS & EQUPMENT ROOM

SERVICE ENTRY

MAIN HALL

HALLWAY

BATH

LIVING QUARTERS

BATH

FLOOR PLAN DRAWING OF DE WIGMORE CASTLE

Mortimer's Cross, Middle Marsh, Wales
from February 1468
© 2010, Clarence W. Padgett

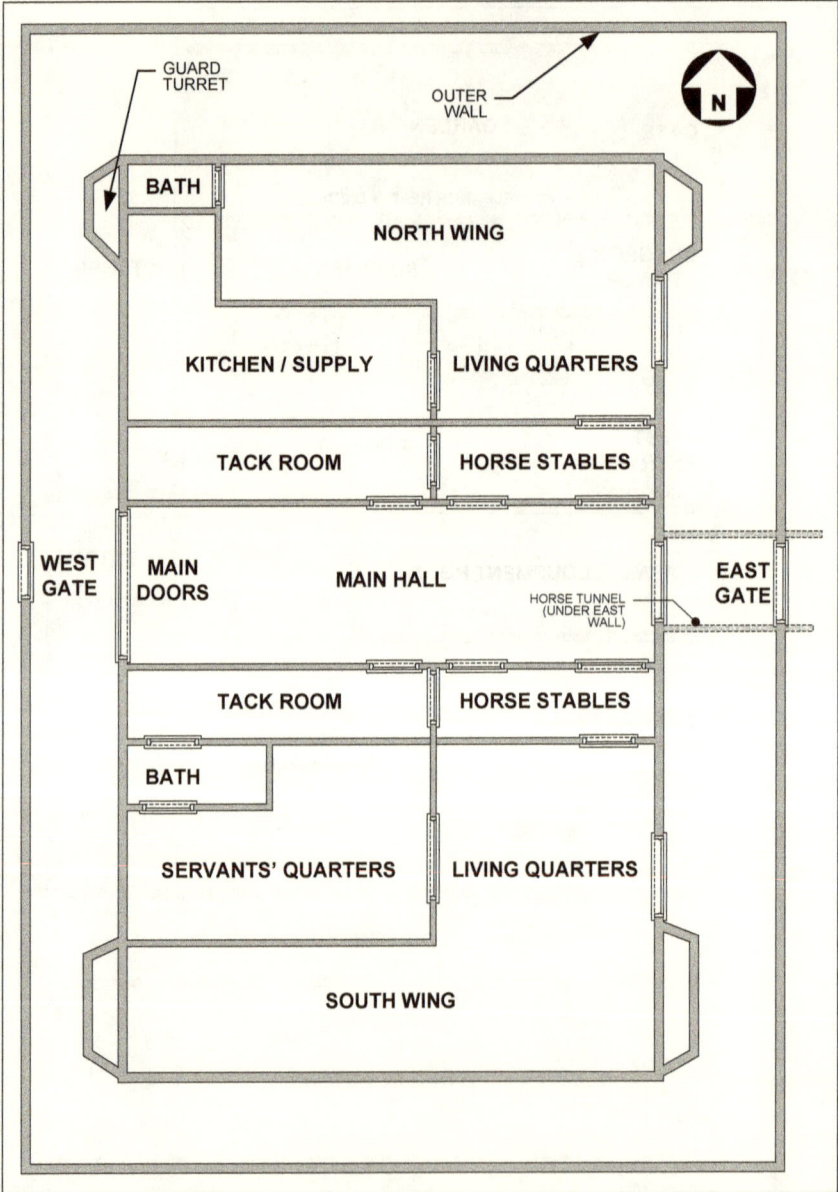

GUARD TURRET

OUTER WALL

N

BATH

NORTH WING

KITCHEN / SUPPLY

LIVING QUARTERS

TACK ROOM

HORSE STABLES

WEST GATE

MAIN DOORS

MAIN HALL

EAST GATE

HORSE TUNNEL (UNDER EAST WALL)

TACK ROOM

HORSE STABLES

BATH

SERVANTS' QUARTERS

LIVING QUARTERS

SOUTH WING

RECORDS OF EDWARD DE WIGMORE / ELEANOR

Eleanor Talbot
F, #107608, d. 1468
Last Edited = 1 May 2002

> Eleanor Talbot died in 1468.
> She was also known as Eleanor Butler.

Child of Eleanor Talbot and Edward IV Plantagenet, King of England.

> 1. Edward de Wigmore b. c 1467, d. 1468

Citations:

> 1. Alison Weir, *Britain's Royal Family: a Complete Geneology* (The Bodley Head: London, UK. 1999), p. 141. Hereafter cited as *Britain's Royal Family*.

Source: *thepeerage.com* retrieved 22 December 2016

Edward de Wigmore
M, #107607, d. 1468
Last Edited = 22 May 2004

Edward de Wigmore was the son of Edward IV Plantagenet, King of England and Eleanor Talbot. He died in 1468, in infancy.

Source: *thepeerage.com* retrieved 2010

Edward de Wigmore
M, #107607, b. circa 1467, d. 1468
Last edited = 22 Jan 2011

> Edward de Wigmore was born illegitimately circa 1467. He was the son of Edward IV Plantagenet, King of England and Eleanor Talbot. He died in 1468, in infancy.

Citations:

> 1. Alison Weir, *Britain's Royal Family: a Complete Geneology* (The Bodley Head: London, UK. 1999), p. 141. Hereafter cited as *Britain's Royal Family*.

Source: *thepeerage.com* retrieved 22 December 2016

Edward de Wigmore

Born: ?
Father: Edward IV of England
Mother: Lady Eleanor Talbot
Children 1: Died at birth with his mother 1468.
Buried: ?
Last modified, 04/04/2010.

Source: *rootsweb.ancestry.com* retrieved 2012

LETTER FROM CARMELITE CHURCH IN ENGLAND

CARMEL OF OUR LADY OF WALSINGHAM
LANGHAM, NORFOLK
NR 25 7BP
Phone: 01328 830 373
Fax: 01328 830 900
email: carmmonlangham@tiscali.co.uk

March 12, 2003

Dear Mr Padgett,

Thank you for your letter enquiring about Lady Eleanor Butler who, you thought, was a nun at a Carmelite Monastery in Norwich in 1468. I myself did not know, except I was pretty sure there were no monasteries of nuns until later. But I contacted the sister who is the unofficial archivist of the nuns in this country and the following is her reply:

Yes, there was a Carmelite house at Norwich, founded in 1256, only a few years after the first house at Aylesford in 1242. However, since Carmelite nuns weren't "invented" till 1452 (witness the celebration of the document "Cum Nulla" of which we are invited to remember the 550th anniversary, and Bl. John Soreth, etc etc this year!) the Lady Eleanor of your Canadian enquirer can hardly have been a nun there.... However, Fr Joe Chalmers O Carm in his recent booklet /letter to the Order, "Into the Land of Carmel" says that the ancient Order were very free and creative in considering lay people , and women, as part of the Carmelite family , just as a matter of devotion, without any canonical status. The "Cum Nulla " thing just regularised the whole business. The Lady in question might have been a devout client or patron of the said Carmelite Friars at Norwich, and maybe buried in their Church, or something like that?? That is just my guess.

Having said that, I hasten to add that there are no longer any Carmelite Friars or Nuns in Norwich itself. In Norfolk there is a monastery at Quidenham and ourselves but neither of us is older than mid-twentieth century! I am not aware, either, of a Carmelite church in Norwich and can find no reference to it. But you may perhaps be able to pursue that if you are on the internet.

Someone at the Carmelite Friary at Aylesford, Kent, ME20 7BX, UK may be able to help you. Most communities have someone who is interested in the history of the Order.

Sorry not to be more help - it is fun to sleuth around though isn't it?

Sincerely,

Sister Judith Leckie, Prioress   (originally from Vancouver).

TITULUS REGIUS (EXCERPT)

The following excerpt from the *Titulus Regius* declares the marriage of King Edward IV to Elizabeth Grey to be illegal and adulterous, and their children to be bastards. In part, this is because Edward had made a precontract of matrimony with "Dame Elianor Butteler" [*sic*] long before the "pretensed" marriage with Elizabeth.

"Over this, amonges other thinges, more specifially we consider howe that the tyme of the raigne of King Edward IV, late decessed, after the ungracious pretensed marriage, as all England hath cause to say, made betwitx the said King edward IV and Elizabeth, sometyme wife to Sir John Grey, Knight, late nameing herself and many years heretofore Queene of England, the ordre of all politeque rule was perverted, the laws of God and of Gode's church, and also the lawes of nature, and of England, and also the laudable customes and liberties of the same, wherein every Englishman is inheritor, broken, subverted, and contempned, against all reason and justice, so that this land was ruled by self-will and pleasure, feare and drede, all manner of equite and lawes layd apart and despised, whereof ensued many inconvenients and mischiefs, as murdres, estortions, and oppressions, namely of pooe and impotent people, so that no man was sure of his lif, land, ne lyuvelode, ne of his wif, doughter, no servannt, every good maiden and woman standing in drede to be ravished and defouled. And besides this, what discords, inward battailes, effusion of Christian men's blode, and namely, by the destruction of the noble blode of this lond, was had and comitted within the same, it is evident and notarie through all this reaume unto the grete sorrowe and heavynesse of all true Englishmen. And here also we considre howe the said pretensed marriage, betwitx the above named King Edward the Elizabeth Grey, was made of grete presumption, without the knowyng or assent of the lords of this londe, and alsoe by sorcerie and wiche-crafte, committed by the said Elizabeth and her moder, Jacquett Duchess of Bedford, as the common opinion of the peole and the publique voice, and fame is through all this land; and hereafter, if and as the case shall require, shall bee proved sufficiently intyme and place convenient. And here also we considre how that the said pretenced marriage was made privately and secretly, with edition of banns, in a private chamber, a profane place, and not openly in the face of the church, aftre the laws of Godd's churche, but contrarie thereunto, and the laudable custome of the Churche of England. And how also, that at the tyme of the contract of the same pretensed marriage, and bifore and longe tyme after, the saide King Edw was and stood marryed and troth plyght to oone Dame Elianor Butteler, doughter of the old Earl of Shrewsbury, with whom the said King Edward had made a precontracte of matronie, long tyme bifore he made the said pretensed mariage with the said Elizabeth Grey in manner and fourme aforesaid. Which premises being true, as in veray trouth they been true, it appeareth and followeth evidently, that the said King Edward duryng his lyfe and the said Elizabeth lived together sinfully and dampnably in adultery, against the lawe of God and his church; and therefore noe marvaile that the souverain lord and head of this londe, being of such ungodly disposicion, and provokyng the ire and indignation of oure Lorde God, such haynous mischiefs and inconvenients as is above remember, were used and committed in the reame amongst the subjects. Also it appeareth evidently and followeth that all th'issue and children of the said king been bastards, and unable to inherite or to clayme anything by inheritance, by the lawe and custome of England."

Source: *http://www.richardiii.com/titulus_regius.htm* retrieved 21 February 2017.

Index

C

K

L

M

S

T

V

W

Y

About The Author

In the early '70s, Padgett wrote two poetry books, *Dog Days Poems* and *Horse's Nose Poems*. He and his wife Sie took the first book of poetry all the way across Canada to Nova Scotia and back selling the first 1,000 copies to cover a summers worth of travel and promotion.

Padgett had worked as an insurance underwriter and had also taken a B.A. degree in history. Even with that experience, he still felt a longing to return to the farming roots he had grown up with. As a result, he and Sie came to the Atnarko Valley in British Columbia, where they lived rent-free for 15 years in exchange for turning an old eighty-acre property into a horse farm. After the farm was sold, the Padgett family moved down into the Bella Coola Valley, where he and Sie reside still.

In 2014, Padgett wrote *The Atnarko Writings*, an expression of some of the history, people and events he and his family experienced while living in the Atnarko Valley.

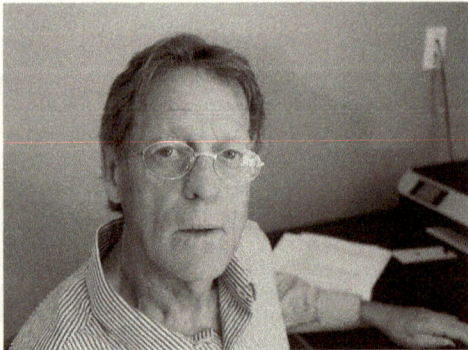

In 1994, Padgett began to experience the series of lucid dreams that compelled him to embark on the journey of discovery that produced this latest book, *A Dream Within A Dream*.